Small Groups

for the End-time

Books by Kurt W. Johnson

LifeLine Bible Study Guides, books 1 and 2
Small Groups for the End-time

A practical guide for the twenty-first century

Small Groups for the End-time

Kurt W. Johnson

REVIEW AND HERALD® PUBLISHING ASSOCIATION
HAGERSTOWN, MD 21740

The author assumes full responsibility for the accuracy of all facts and quotations as cited in this book.

This book was
Edited by Tim Crosby
Copyedited by Jocelyn Fay and James Cavil
Cover design by Genesis Design/Bryan Gray
Cover photos by PhotoDisc
Typeset: 11.5/13.5 Times

PRINTED IN U.S.A.

01 00 99 98 97 5 4 3 2 1

R&H Cataloging Service
Johnson, Kurt Wayne, 1950-
Small groups for the end-time.

1. Church group work. I. Title.

253.7

ISBN 0-8280-1315-2

Contents

Chapter One

The Bones Are Rattling

I was having fun that warm, sunny afternoon. It was the kind of day when a boy enjoys being a boy. The flies were buzzing around my head, and perspiration trickled down my face from running and playing. A fly landed on my face. I swatted at it but received a sting on my cheek for the effort. No matter; I was having fun. I ducked under the barnyard fence and made my way across the pasture, pretending that the cows were bandits and I was a cowboy riding my horse across the open plain. I stopped my imaginary horse now and then and looked around to make sure no bandits were lurking behind the rocks, then carefully moved on.

As I neared the end of the pasture, I stopped abruptly. There in front of me was a disjointed animal skeleton. I reached down and picked up one of the bones and turned it over in my hands. It was white-gray and rough, like sandpaper. I wondered if it had been a deer or a cow? Whatever it was, it once had life, energy, and a purpose for living.

Now the bones were dry, brittle, disintegrating, almost dust—almost forgotten. I stood there, turning the bone over in my hands, muttering, "I wonder . . . ?"

A Valley Full of Bones

It appears as if the war is over and the enemy is forever defeated. Satan gloats as he looks upon the scene. *I won*, he thinks. *I've beaten Jesus and His church!* Before him, the barren mountains loom up on each side of the vast desert floor. A lone vulture circles, dips down toward the ground, and then rises and moves on. A lizard, with flicking tongue, pauses momentarily beside one of the scattered plants that barely cling to life. The temperature at midday drives even the scavengers in search of shelter from the oppressive heat.

It is not an enjoyable sight. Skeletons of men, women, and children lie in heaps, scattered across the open plain. The bones lie bleached and cracked in the sun. But in this ghastly scene God has a message for His church.

We read about it in Ezekiel 37:1-4: "The hand of the Lord came upon me and brought me out in the Spirit of the Lord, and set me down in the midst of the valley; and it was full of bones. Then He caused me to pass by them all around, and behold, there were very many in the open valley; and indeed they were very dry. And He said to me, 'Son of man, can these bones live?' So I answered, 'O Lord God, You know.' Again He said to me, 'Prophesy to these bones, and say to them, "O dry bones, hear the word of the Lord!" ' " (NKJV).

"Son of man, can these bones live?"

I stood alone in the pasture. The bleached bone in my hand had begun to crack and splinter. Once it had been soft and full of marrow. Now it had no life. Even if I soaked it in water like the roots of a plant, there would still be no life. Even if I sent the bone to the hospital for a bone marrow transplant, there still would be no life. Even if someone transplanted the bone into a living animal, there would be no life. The bone would still be dry and lifeless.

If God had asked me the question He asked Ezekiel, "Can these bones live?" my answer would have been "No, Lord, it is impossible. Soon the bones will return to dust and be forgotten."

Ezekiel goes on to explain that the dry, lifeless bones represent God's people. They are discouraged as they survey their present condition. They say, "Our bones are dry, our hope is lost, and we ourselves are cut off!" (verse 11). In contrast is the healthy, Spirit-filled church of 1 Corinthians 12. There the church is compared to a human body, with Christ as the head, and the members of the church—the rest of the body—in proper connection with Him. The skeletal parts are attached to one another; there are sinews, muscles, and tendons. The organs are healthy and function optimally for maximum performance.

What a difference between this ideal and the sad picture of God's people in Ezekiel! One group working harmoniously to fulfill God's will; the other Spiritless and lifeless, so that even the vultures find nothing to feast on!

Paul amplifies God's desire for His church by stating in Ephesians 4:11-16 that the leaders are to prepare the members of the body for service (verses 11, 12). Why?

- To build up the body (verse 12).
- To assist the members in obtaining unity of faith (verse 13).
- To assist the body in growing in their understanding of who Jesus is (verse 13).
- To become mature members of the body (verse 13).
- To attain a lifestyle like that of Jesus (verse 13).
- To become fully connected to Jesus Christ in all aspects of daily life (verse 13).

The result of this is that "The whole body, joined and held together by every supporting ligament, grows and builds itself up in love, as each part does its work" (verse 16, NIV). This passage makes it clear, I believe, that the church is intended to be a dynamic organism, growing numerically and relationally.

Ezekiel's description is a sad one. A church cut off is a people with no vision or commitment to a mission. The members have stopped seeking and saving the lost. They have forgotten the church's mission and reason for existence: to save those who will go into Christless graves unless someone tells them about Jesus!

A dead church is a church that cannot see beyond the sin problems of the individual members and leaders to a perfect Saviour, Jesus Christ. The politics, gossiping, criticism, and lack of forgiveness leave the members in bondage to Satan, so they are forced to try to do ministry on their own, using manipulative methods.

A church of dry bones is a people not being daily renewed and filled with the Holy Spirit; not growing in their relationship with Jesus. Daily personal Bible study, prayer, family worship, scripture memorization, and united seeking of the Spirit are rare. The members have forgotten that Jesus said, "You will receive power when the Holy Spirit comes on you" (Acts 1:8, NIV). They have forgotten that they receive power by being in His presence.

Ezekiel 37 is a sad commentary on the state of the elect. The people portrayed there are without direction and life. Such people have forgotten their reason for being; forgotten the power of the gospel; forgotten how to be continually empowered. They have form and structure, a skeletal system—an organization—but it is of little worth. Why? Because the delivery system is powerless. It is void of the Holy Spirit.

Ezekiel gives a prophecy of hope! God says, "I will cause breath to enter into you, and you shall live. . . . Then you shall know that I am the Lord" (verses 5, 6, NKJV). Then Ezekiel describes the bones coming together, and the sinews, muscles, organs, flesh, and skin covering the skeletal structure. There is now form and structure, but this is not enough. Until God gives breath to the newly formed body and stands it on its feet, there is no power. Without the breath of God the structure is only a mere form, a dry skeleton.

God's Solution

Once again I seem to stand alone in the pasture staring at the dry bones of an animal. I hear God's question to Ezekiel, "Can these bones live?" I respond this time, "Yes, Lord, You can make them live again." But how are these dry bones to be revived? How are the disintegrated bones of the church to live again? How does the revived, empowered army accomplish its mission of possessing "the land"?

God answers and says, "I will put My Spirit in you, and you shall live, and I will place you in your own land. Then you shall know that I, the Lord, have spoken it and performed it" (verse 14). Notice the emphasis on God's initiative. God has a vision of His church—you, me—in partnership with Him.

George Barna, in his book *The Power of Vision*, describes vision as:

- seeing the invisible and making it visible.
- a dream with wheels and a road map.[1]

In his book *My Utmost for His Highest* Oswald Chambers describes vision this way: "God gives us the vision, then He takes us down to the valley to alter us into the shape of the vision, and it is in the valley that so many of us faint and give way. Every vision will be made real if we will have patience."[2]

A vision is something that works on our lives and in our lives, not something we work on. No one ever attains the vision, but we live in the inspiration of it until God accomplishes it. Vision is a passion, a calling, a drive or compulsion that simply will not let us go. We talk about the need to "catch the vision." But the type of vision that God wants us to have is not caught; it catches us.[3]

Vision alters us. One cannot remain the same while gripped by a vision. It is impossible! Think about those in the Bible whom God used to make a difference. They all had to be transformed and revived by God before they were willing and able to be a part of Christ's vision. This is a critical point: *they did not do God's vision; they were altered by the vision so God could accomplish His will through them.*

God said . . .

- Adam and Eve, even though you sinned, there is hope. Through your seed I will redeem you and the world.
- Abraham, your seed will be as the stars of the heavens. But if I am to use you, you must leave your homeland, which you love, and go to the land to which I tell you to go.
- Moses, you will set My people free and lead them to Canaan. But first, go herd sheep for 40 years.
- David, you are My chosen king. There are some rough spots in your character that need work; but you are a man after My own heart.
- Mary, I know that the moralists look down on your past, but I have a unique work for you. Trust Me and walk in this vision.
- Paul, I need your passion. But to use it I need to get your attention—I may have to strike you temporarily blind so that you can really see. After that I will be able to use you!

Our human approach is to say, "I believe this is God's vision for me, so now I will get busy and do it—watch me!" This is natural and normal, but it is not right. When we are changed by God, we are no longer concerned about our vision, but we wait for God to shape us to fill our part of His vision. Being a part of God's vision can be costly—Jesus told us that it may cost us family, friends, houses and lands, and even our freedom. In fact, if the vision is unclear and we have not been altered and shaped by the Spirit to fit God's vision, the cost will be too high. When the going gets tough, and the waves start rolling, those who don't have a strong commitment to the vision will bail out of the boat.[4]

This past Memorial Day I walked through the cemetery to place flowers on my dad's grave. I was familiar with the cemetery and quickly found the headstone. I stood for a while and thought about all of those buried there. God's desire is to raise them from their graves and to stand them on their feet and give them life. He wants to breathe His Spirit into them and make them part of His great army to take to the kingdom. It should be the number one passion of your life and mine to add to that number who will be ready when Jesus comes.

We also need to walk through another cemetery—Ezekiel's valley—and look at the dry bones of our own lives and our own congregation. Sometimes I have tried to rattle the old bones myself. Sometimes we try to figure out what sinew and muscle ingredients are needed to hold the bones together. But our list of essentials may be more human than divine. Let's journey together through the pages of this book and together try to glimpse God's vision.

You need to know up front that this may be a costly venture. To follow Jesus is to die. Following Him may mean putting to death our own agendas, programs, and well-intentioned dreams. If we are willing to be shaped by Him, He will give life to our dry bones.[5]

---

[1] George Barna, *The Power of Vision* (Ventura, Calif: Regal Books, 1992), pp. 28-41.

[2] Oswald Chambers, *My Utmost for His Highest* (New York: Dodd, Mead and Co., 1961), pp. 188, 71.

[3] William Beckham, *The Second Reformation* (Houston: Touch Publications, 1995), p. 23.

[4] *Ibid.,* chap. 21.

[5] *Ibid.*

Chapter Two

Lone Ranger Christians

It is time to change some of the ways we do church. Not every way, of course. We are doing many things right. But let's look at both sides of the issue. First, what are we doing right?

The Global Mission project of the Adventist Church is bringing thousands of people to accept Jesus. Much of this is being accomplished through the laity. In 1996 more than 2,000 new congregations were established, and 659,899 men and women became members of the Seventh-day Adventist Church around the world. In China alone, 114 churches were established in areas each with a population of one million people where five years before we did not have even one member.[1]

The Global Mission Pioneer work of the church is exciting! Lay members are committing their lives as modern day "tentmakers" to plant new churches. As I write:

- There are 200 pioneers in India.
- Indonesia has 150 target sites for new churches, and a goal of training and sending 300 pioneers throughout India.
- Russia currently has 100 pioneers in service.
- The Ivory Coast has 45 pioneers.
- All over the world, including North America, students are committing their lives to mission service.

The methods used are many—literature evangelism, literacy programs, health seminars, Vacation Bible Schools, Bible studies, small group house meetings, visitation, and much more.

The stories are also exciting!

- In India the wife of one of the literature evangelists is a tailor. By looking for opportunities to talk about Jesus, she has seen 10 customers baptized.
- In New Guinea a pioneer church planter has been stoned, attacked with guns and machetes, and had his literature set on fire. The result has been 10 baptisms and 16 recent decisions for baptism. The new church planting effort has been successful.[2]
- In Russia the outreach work has exploded! The baptismal growth rate, planting of new churches, the establishment of Sabbath school Action Units and home fellowship groups, along with other methods, has resulted in unprecedented growth for the Euro-Asia Division.
- In North America NET '95 and NET '96 have sparked a resurgence in evangelism.

The Spirit of God is moving throughout the world, and we are thankful! These are some of the ways we as Adventist Church members are doing ministry right. But now let's look at some of the problems with the mission of the church.

Studies reveal that approximately 80 percent of church attendees in North America are consumers—they attend church once a week while the remaining 20 percent are involved in ministry weekly—the familiar 80/20 rule.[3]

There are about 300 million people living in North America. Only 1 million of them are Seventh-day Adventists. Approximately half of all non-Adventists do not even recognize the name Seventh-day Adventist, or if they do they confuse Adventists with other religious groups.[4]

The average Adventist church in North America spends only 5 percent of its budget on evangelism to the community, but 30 percent of its budget on buildings and maintenance.[5]

If your church is more than 15 years old you can expect three new converts each year for every 100 members. But if your church is less than three years old you can expect 10 converts for every 100 members. That is why between 80 and 85 percent of all churches in North America are declining in membership. Roger Dudley, an Adventist researcher at Andrews University, tells us that new Adventist churches grow at 10 times the rate of established churches.[6]

A recent study of 1,700 Adventists showed that half of them had five or fewer non-Adventist friends. We cannot reach those we do not know![7]

Some church members see the pastor as one who meets the needs of the sick and discouraged; visits and gives Bible studies to the non-

Christians; chairs meetings; manages the finances of the church; and preaches a sermon each week that meets the spiritual and emotional needs of the congregation. If a church elder or another member performs the ministry function, it's "not the same"—we need the pastor to be there. Is this a realistic understanding of the pastor's role?

We are constantly developing programs to stem the tide of nonattending members and to "lock the back door of the church" so the newly baptized don't leave. The search for a contemporary solution is a constant and frustrating struggle—so we are tempted to "constructively" criticize the methods, the pastor, the evangelist, the spiritual guardian, or the conference.

In many churches a member may be absent for several weeks without being noticed or contacted. Recently a man in church told me that he visited a person the previous week who hadn't attended the local church during the past year. He was told that only one person in the church (who had been a close friend) still contacted him periodically.

Studies reveal that a new member must develop a minimum of seven close friends in the church during the first year of their joining, or they will probably stop attending. I know that we as church members care. How can we do it better?

Jesus said, "The harvest is plentiful . . . ask the Lord of the harvest therefore to send out workers" (Luke 10:2, NIV). Where will we find these reapers? Only 3 to 10 percent of the members in the local church are consistently involved in overt evangelism (Bible studies, outreach small groups, visitation, etc.) or ministry that is directed specifically to non-Christians. Why?

According to the United Nations Population Division, every year the equivalent of another Mexico—nearly 100 million people—is added to the world's population.

Statisticians tell us that the world population in Jesus' time equaled the United States population in 1995. By Martin Luther's time the population doubled. This took 1,500 years. Three hundred years later, in the early 1800s, the population doubled again, and again in 1930. From 1930 to 2000, a 70-year period, it will skyrocket to 6.5 billion and then double again in the early twenty-first century.[8] That is a lot of people who need to know Jesus!

Since there are more Christians than ever before, why are we making so little headway? And what are you going to do about it?

Breaking Out of the Cocoon

Too many Christians live like the Lone Ranger, who always appeared on the scene at the appropriate moment to solve the dilemma. No one knew who the Lone Ranger was in everyday life. He seemed to need no one (besides Tonto), and faced life all alone. Whenever there was a crisis, he was there, and then—*poof*—he rode off into the sunset.

That is how some Christians live. They hide away from one another except for Sabbath. The rest of the week they are wrapped up in jobs, household duties, a church meeting once in a while, and their own group of friends. They rarely have time for prayer meeting, a weekly small group, individual Bible studies, friendship evangelism, or other ministry. Periodically when an announcement is made in church about an emergency need they drop everything and help, then retreat back into their own cocoon. A few years ago the author of the book *Megatrends* called this a high-tech/low-touch society.[9]

Cocooning is a buzzword of the nineties. It refers to those who prefer to hide away from the rest of society, too tired to do anything but "crash" at home. An interesting result of this trend is seen in a recent study to determine which pizza consumers liked the best and which one had the highest sales volume. Interestingly, Pizza Hut pizza was the favorite in taste, but Domino's pizza had the largest sales volume. Why? Because Domino's delivers and Pizza Hut, for the most part, doesn't. The consumer is willing to take "second best" in order to stay at home and be insulated from society.[10]

Church must be more than what happens one day of the week. A church must go beyond its parking lot and become a loving community where Christians are nurtured, and those not knowing Christ are reached with the gospel. The Scriptures are plain:

- "Go therefore and make disciples of all the nations, baptizing them in the name of the Father and of the Son and of the Holy Spirit" (Matt. 28:19, NKJV).
- "And this gospel of the kingdom will be preached in all the world as a witness to all the nations, and then the end will come" (Matt. 24:14, NKJV).
- There are diversities of gifts, differences of ministry, but each person is given a manifestation of the Spirit (a ministry or something to do for Jesus) (see 1 Cor. 12:4-7).

Some Christians hide behind their spiritual gifts as an excuse to avoid witnessing. "Well," they say, "my gift is to play the piano in the children's division, so I don't need to become acquainted with my non-Christian neighbors or work associates." But God has called us to witness. If not you, then who? That does not mean that you must always be giving individual

Bible studies or presenting the gospel to unbelievers. But it does mean that you make yourself available as a friend. Let God provide the opportunity to talk to them about Jesus. If you need assistance with explaining the Bible or the gospel, there are plenty of Christians to help you. But unless every Christian is concerned about the eternal salvation of those with whom they come in contact, many will go down into Christless graves. Perhaps the next victim will be your next-door neighbor or work associate.

A survey revealed that in North America there are 40,000 to 50,000 towns and villages with no Adventist presence. And there are thousands of towns and cities that have a large enough population base to handle numerous churches. We must avoid the fallacy that one church in every town means that we have accomplished our mission for Jesus in that city. If the average membership of a church in North America is approximately 75 to 100 members, and most communities average more than 1,000 in population base—then we need to target sections of the city for planting a new church for Jesus Christ![11]

Ellen White was very bold and visionary in her comments.

"Missionaries are wanted to go into towns and villages, and raise the standard of truth, that God may have His witnesses scattered all over the land, that the light of truth may penetrate where it has not yet reached, and the standard of truth be raised where it is not yet known. . . . Jesus did not neglect the villages. The record declares that 'He went throughout every city and village, preaching and showing the glad tidings of the kingdom of God.'"[12]

"I saw jets of light shining from cities and villages, and from the high places and the low places of the earth. God's Word was obeyed, and as a result there were memorials for Him in every city and village."[13]

As we consider the world situation in which we are called to witness, it is obvious we have a work to do. I do not believe the foundational issue is a spiritual problem—it is a spiritual issue, but not a spiritual problem. Let me explain. I believe that the majority of Christians desire to use their gifts in ministry and to be actively involved in a developing and growing relationship with Jesus. The problem is in the way some of us "do church"—the methods used. Our message and mission are clear and anchored; but we must review our methods.

It is important for us to be purpose-driven; otherwise we are not aiming for targets. The shotgun approach is ineffective—it stings, but does not do the job.

If we are not careful in our methods of outreach and discipleship, we will produce consumer Christians; spectator Christians who will hide in the pew. These are Christians who lack the maturity of the Spirit in their relationship with Jesus, which in turn is reflected in their lifestyle.

In some cases we simply *collect* people and don't *connect* them to other members and involvement in ministry—we give someone Bible studies, baptize them, encourage them to attend church and Sabbath school. If possible, we attempt to get them involved in church life by putting them on the social committee or asking them to join a singing band for the local Ingathering project.

This is not bad, but it is not enough. We can do better! I believe Ellen White and Scripture have given us a foundational approach that has a better chance of helping us to produce fully devoted disciples of Jesus Christ who are involved in outreach from the very beginning of their Christian life. Whatever process one follows (and I believe there is a variety of approaches using similar ingredients), it must produce new believers who are actively involved in using their gifts in ministry in reaching lost people for Jesus. *Just as a mother gives birth naturally, so the new birth experience should give birth naturally to new believers who are active in ministry. They should be birthed in such a manner that the new believer is not even aware that there is any other way to live!*

The church is a movement, not a building; an organism, not an organization. An organism is alive and active. Just as the human body is made up of many cells, which in turn make up the various organs of the body, so the church consists of many members or parts of the body functioning in partnership and unity. For the body of Christ to be healthy, it must have both cells (the smaller component of the church—individual ministry and small groups) and the whole body (large group—worship services, reaping crusades, outreach seminars, etc.) functioning together in ministry.

One key principle to remember is this: the life of the body is in the cell. So in the church, the place where ministry occurs at the optimum is where the individual members can use their spiritual gifts in outreach to others. Our priority must be individual ministry, and not church structures, systems, programs, or church services. As important as these things are, they are not the priority. It is time to empower the laity for ministry. It is time to take another look at the role and function of the pastor and, if necessary, to redefine the role. Yes, it is time to change or adapt the system where necessary so it can give birth naturally to an empowered lay movement!

As Seventh-day Adventists we have a unique mission to the world that includes delivering the end-time message of Revelation 14. We must be bold and yet wise and culturally relevant in our acceptance and carrying out of this task. If you and I don't say "Here am I, Lord, send me," then who will accomplish the mission?

A Tale of Two Cities

In a major city a team from an academy in the Pacific Northwest was conducting lay training meetings for a church of 350 members. After the training it was decided to plant two churches of 70 members each from the home church. Two young pastors were assigned to the two congregations to prepare the members for ministry.

One of the young pastors, knowing this was the challenge and opportunity of a lifetime, decided to use the methods he had learned from the academy team. He had learned how to divide his members into ministry groups, train them, and send them out into the community (Paul in Ephesians 4:12 [NKJV] calls this equipping). The pastor informed his congregation that he didn't know the answers to all of their questions, but he knew there were thousands in the city who needed Jesus in their lives, and he could help them learn how to share Jesus with them. He divided his 70 members into 12 small groups that met together for their Sabbath school class and during the week in the homes of the members. In the home meeting the members invited their friends and family to attend their small group Bible studies. On Sabbath the class studied the lesson and spent time discussing and praying for their own personal needs and for their small group outreach. Within 10 months 49 people were baptized, and the church membership went from 70 to 119. The newly baptized members were already members of a home group, they remained in the group for nurturing and discipleship, and they began inviting their own friends and family to join a home group. Since virtually the entire membership was involved in ministry, the new members thought that was how it was supposed to be, and they became active too.

The second pastor followed a more traditional model of ministry. He visited his members faithfully, he preached excellent sermons, there was a general lesson study on Sabbath, but there were no home small groups, no visitation teams, no outreach Sabbath school classes, or other ministry teams being equipped for service. Within 10 months there was dissension, no baptisms, and a loss of 40 of the original members.[14]

The difference between these two churches was in the equipping of the laity and releasing them to service. God has called us to do the same.

Brad Smith, in an article in the magazine *NEXT*, summarizes the trend today in church life toward equipping the laity in these words: "The church of the twenty-first century will be one that returns to the Ephesians 4 emphasis on equipping lay believers in a fresh way that has not been seen in the United States for decades."[15]

I believe that this trend of lay ministry empowerment is a sign that we are living in the last days of earth's history. In Acts 2, Peter described the first rain of the Holy Spirit at Pentecost as a fulfillment of prophecy, quoting the prophecy of Joel: "And it shall come to pass in the last days, says God, that I will pour out of My Spirit on all flesh; your sons and your daughters shall prophesy, your young men shall see visions, your old men shall dream dreams. And on My menservants and on My maidservants I will pour out My Spirit in those days" (Acts 2:17, 18, NKJV).

In the same way, when the latter rain of the Holy Spirit is poured out, Ellen White describes the scene this way: "In visions of the night, representations passed before me of a great reformatory movement among God's people. Many were praising God. The sick were healed, and other miracles were wrought. A spirit of intercession was seen, even as was manifested before the great Day of Pentecost. Hundreds and thousands were seen visiting families and opening before them the word of God. Hearts were convicted by the power of the Holy Spirit, and a spirit of genuine conversion was manifest. On every side doors were thrown open to the proclamation of the truth. The world seemed to be lightened with the heavenly influence. Great blessings were received by the true and humble people of God. I heard voices of thanksgiving and praise, and there seemed to be a reformation such as we witnessed in 1844."[16]

God has always called His people first to *come* to Him for the filling of the Spirit. Only then does He say *"Go!"* We must not get the order backwards. We can't go and then come, or we will be doing ministry on our own, and we will become discouraged and see pitiful results. We must always *come* first to the feet of Jesus—as He told the disciples to wait at Pentecost for the Holy Spirit. Then we must *go*—ministering to those who need to know Jesus. This is heaven's formula.

The church is doing lots of things right, praise God, but there are things we can do better! As long as we have not accomplished our mission and Jesus has not returned, we must strive for excellence and be open to new methods.

---

[1] *133rd Annual Statistical Report—1995* (General Conference of Seventh-day Adventists); Advertising brochure, Global Mission 1996.

[2] Jackie Ordelheide Smith, coordinator for Global Mission Pioneers, information and

stories from the General Conference Global Mission office, December 1996.

[3] Robert Raines, *New Life in the Church* (New York: Harper and Row, 1961), p. 141.

[4] Alfred C. McClure, Seeds '96 sermon, "We Have Caught the Flame," June 12, 1996. (Condensed version, "Planting and Harvesting," was published in the *Adventist Review,* December 1996.)

[5] *Ibid.*

[6] *Ibid.*

[7] *Ibid.*

[8] W. Beckham, *The Second Reformation,* p. 53. Quoting from "Warm the Storks," Houston *Chronicle,* May 18, 1992.

[9] John Naisbitt and Patricia Aberdene, *Megatrends 2000* (New York: Morrow Publishing, 1990).

[10] Michael Slaughter, Beyond Small Groups Seminar Tapes. (Pasadena, Calif.: Charles E. Fuller Institute), tape 3.

[11] "Reaching Unentered Towns Through NET '96" (Silver Spring, Md.: North American Division of Seventh-day Adventists, 1996), chapter 7, p. 59.

[12] Ellen G. White, *Evangelism* (Washington, D.C.: Review and Herald Pub. Assn., 1946), p. 52.

[13] *Ibid.,* p. 699.

[14] John McGhee, "A Tale of Two Cities," *McGhee Family Newsletter,* Jan. 26, 1996.

[15] Brad Smith, "Team Ministry in the 21st Century," *NEXT,* February 1996, pp. 1-4. Quoted in *Current Thoughts and Trends,* June 1996.

[16] E. G. White, *Testimonies for the Church* (Mountain View, Calif.: Pacific Press Pub. Assn., 1948), vol. 9, p. 126.

Chapter Three

The Poison That Caused the Reformation

Hanford Nuclear Reservation is causing great concern in the northwestern United States. During the 1940s and 1950s, low-level nuclear waste from Hanford's reactors and processing facilities typically was held in open lagoons or dumped directly on the ground, where it contaminated the groundwater. Eventually the waste was stored in sealed containers and buried. Today there are 177 massive underground tanks holding a total of 61 million gallons of deadly atomic poisons.

However, the barrels are beginning to leak. The liquids are seeping out and slowly nearing the aqueducts that flow into the mighty Columbia River, posing a serious threat to the fish and other aquatic life, and to those who depend on the river for drinking water and irrigation. There is little time left to act before it is too late.[1]

There are other types of poison that cause problems for society. Satan does his best to insidiously infiltrate the mind. He uses entertainment, advertising media, and books and videos as avenues into the souls of men and women. Satan also attacks the church. Jesus said the devil goes about as a roaring lion seeking those to devour (1 Peter 5:8). He is the great deceiver (Matt. 24:24); a thief and a robber who sneaks into the flock to destroy the sheep (John 10:1-18).

Why are these terms used? Because Satan does not want the men and women walking the streets of the cities of this world to come to know Jesus as Lord and Saviour of their lives.

It is interesting to examine the tactics that Satan uses to destroy God's people:

- Herod tried to kill Jesus at His birth.
- After Jesus' baptism, Satan tried to trap Him by tempting Him to bow down and give allegiance to Satan.
- Several attempts were made on Jesus' life while He was on this earth.
- Jesus died on the cross—an apparent victory for Satan that turned out to be a great victory for Christians and a complete defeat for Satan.
- Paul and others persecuted Christians of the fledgling church.

Not only does Scripture demonstrate Satan's desire to eliminate Christianity, but historians document how the Roman Empire cooperated in this process.

Nero, a first-century Roman emperor, passed decrees with the intent of inhibiting certain new movements and secret societies, stating that Christians could not build churches or public meeting places. Violators could lose their property, Roman citizenship, and even their lives.[2] This is one of the reasons that Christians first met in their homes for worship. Nero unwittingly assisted in establishing an outreach system that defeated his own desire to restrict the growth of Christianity.

Nero became a relentless persecutor. He set fire to Rome, perhaps to clear space for his new building projects, and then blamed it on the Christians.[3] He had animal skins sewn around Christians who refused to denounce their faith, and as cheering spectators watched, the martyrs were ripped to pieces by wild dogs.[4] Nero's fame as a persecutor, however, was assured when he became the first emperor to ride a chariot through his private gardens by the light of human torches! He had the Christian martyrs covered with oily tar and then set on fire for his enjoyment.[5]

Nero's decree against church buildings lasted some 250 years (A.D. 64-313), but the church continued to grow anyway, meeting in homes.[6]

Trajan, the Roman emperor from A.D. 98 to 117, revived the decrees against secret societies. Included in his list was Christianity, which he labeled a "depraved and immoderate superstition." Consequently, the persecution the church had faced under the preceding emperor, Domitian, continued for some Christians who met and worshiped together.[7]

Finally, the Roman emperor Constantine brought persecution to a halt in A.D. 313 by making Christianity the legal religion of the Roman Empire. Constantine built a number of cathedrals.[8] It was at this time that the church's theology and practice began to shift regarding the role and function of the laity. John Wesley recognized this progression centuries later. He said, "Even in the first century the mystery of iniquity began to work in the church, culminating with the baptism of the Emperor

Constantine, productive of far more evil to the church than all the ten persecutions put together. For at that time the church and state, the kingdoms of Christ and of the world, were so strangely and unnaturally blended together . . . that they will hardly ever be divided till Christ comes to reign upon earth."[9]

Some of the doctrinal weeds that sprang up during the dark ages of church history spawned the seeds of the Reformation. The Reformers reacted against the poison being insidiously forced upon the Christian church. Martin Luther nailed his ninety-five theses on the door of the church in Wittenberg, Germany. He and other fathers of the Reformation began to call the church back to Scripture as the sole authority for belief and practice. Martin Luther dealt with such theological issues as baptism, salvation through the gift of Jesus Christ, Christ as our direct mediator, etc. Seventh-day Adventists would add to the list the clarification of the Sabbath, state of the dead, and the sanctuary message as other key doctrines that needed theological attention. But the area we wish to focus on is the involvement of the laity in ministry.

When Constantine declared Christianity to be the official religion of the Roman Empire and gave permission for churches to be built (A.D. 313), the theology of the church changed. As will be seen in a later chapter, the members of the early church primarily met in their homes for their religious gatherings because they had no church buildings. The apostles and other leading disciples (equivalent to our paid clergy today) were primarily church planters, equippers of the laity for ministry, and circuit-riding preachers. Elders were appointed in the churches to do the work of overseeing the members and outreach. The elders and deacons took care of the basic everyday needs of the church members. Public meetings were evidently held in houses, with attendance from a handful to more than 100. The Scriptures refer to house churches and mention that the disciples went from house to house. Ministry was by the elders, deacons, and other church members. The pastors were evangelists and administrators ("overseers").

The construction of church buildings for public corporate worship under Constantine had advantages and disadvantages. In the newly constructed basilicas the people attended church services at least once a week. A pastor or priest instructed them and directed the worship service. The ministry needs of the members were met by the pastor. Some members may have felt that corporate worship fulfilled their ministry obligation. Since Constantine, the church has never been the same.

Adventist Church Life

In the early days of the Seventh-day Adventist Church we followed a model of church life that was closer to the early church methodology. C. Mervyn Maxwell refers to a newspaper interview by a reporter with G. B. Starr during an evangelistic campaign. This article sheds light on the Adventist model of ministry in our church's formative years. Starr was asked by what means the Adventists had grown so rapidly. His answer:

"We have no settled pastors. Our churches are taught largely to take care of themselves, while nearly all of our ministers work as evangelists in new fields. In the winter they go out into the churches, halls, or school house and raise up believers. In the summer we use tents, pitching them in the cities and villages where we teach the people these doctrines. This year we shall run about 100 tents in this way. Besides these, we send out large numbers of colporteurs with our tracts and books, who visit the families and teach them the Bible. Last year we employed about 125 in this manner. Bible reading is another class of work. The workers go from house to house holding Bible readings with from one to twenty individuals. Last year they gave 10,000 of such Bible readings. At the same time we had employed about 300 canvassers, constantly canvassing the country and selling our larger works. In addition to this every church has a missionary society. Last year these numbered 10,500 members. Every one of these members does more or less missionary work, such as selling books, loaning or giving away tracts, obtaining subscriptions to our periodicals, visiting families, looking after the poor, aiding the sick, etc. Last year they made 102,000 visits, wrote 40,000 letters, obtained 38,700 subscriptions to our periodicals, distributed 15,500,000 pages of reading matter and 1,600,000 periodicals."[10]

No wonder the Adventist Church grew! We might not use exactly the same methods today, but the principle is the same—an involved and empowered laity. Ellen White writes, "To every one work has been allotted, and no one can be a substitute for another."[11]

At a ministerial meeting in Los Angeles, California, in March 1912, A. G. Daniells, General Conference president, spoke these words:

"We have not settled our ministers over churches as pastors to any large extent. In some of the very large churches we have elected pastors, but as a rule we have held ourselves ready for field service, evangelistic work, and our brethren and sisters have held themselves ready to maintain their church services and carry forward their church work without settled pastors. And I hope this will never cease to be the order of affairs in this denomination; for when we cease our forward movement work and begin to settle over our churches, to stay by them, and do their thinking and their praying and their work that is to be done, then our churches will begin to weaken, and to lose their life and spirit, and become paralyzed and fossilized and our work will be on a retreat."[12]

Paralyzed and fossilized—those words remind me of Ezekiel's "valley of dry bones" with which we began this book. A church that is inactive in ministry is a church that is dead or dying. A church that depends solely on the pastor and the leaders chosen by the nominating committee to do their ministry for them is a church that is out of harmony with God's will. As Seventh-day Adventists we would not think of violating the Sabbath hours by improper activity, but some have fallen into Satan's trap of ignoring God's plan of taking the gospel to all the world. That plan involves every Christian involved in ministry at all times. The Bible calls this constant readiness "in season and out of season" (2 Timothy 4:2, NIV).

The first 39 pages of *Testimonies for the Church,* volume 7, highlight the way the Adventist Church grew in its first 60 years. Here was the methodology on which the growth was based:

"Just as soon as a church is organized, let the minister set the members at work. They will need to be taught how to labor successfully."[13]

"The greatest help that can be given our people is to teach them to work for God, and to depend on Him, not on the ministers."[14]

"God has not given His ministers the work of setting the churches right. No sooner is this work done, apparently, than it has to be done over again. Church members that are thus looked after and labored for become religious weaklings. . . . God has withheld His blessings because His people have not worked in harmony with His directions."[15]

"Churches are to be organized, and plans laid for work to be done by the members of the newly organized churches. As workers go forth filled with zeal, and with the love of God, the churches at home will be revived; for the success of the workers will be regarded as a subject of deep personal concern by every member of the church."[16]

Some of us have lost our passion for those who need to know Jesus. It is so easy to get caught up in the whirlwind of life that we forget our reason for being. Too many of us have left ministry to the paid clergy—we pay our tithe, so the pastor can reach the lost, and we drive off to our places of employment thinking we have done our part. That mind-set is not biblical and must be changed! We must think this way: *God has given me an occupation to earn money to sustain my family, but my occupation is primarily my field of ministry. The money is secondary; lost people are primary!* This does not mean that one does not respect the rights and privacy of clientele or customers, but it does mean that each of us must pray for and look for opportunities to make a spiritual difference in the lives of men and women in our community.

Spiritual Gifts

In chapter one we briefly touched on Ephesians 4. In his statement on spiritual gifts Paul describes God's method of accomplishing nurture and outreach ministry. In verse 7 we are told that God has something for every Christian to do in ministry: "But to each one of us grace was given according to the measure of Christ's gift" (NKJV). Paul says the same thing in 1 Corinthians 12:4-7: "the manifestation of the Spirit is given to each one" (NKJV). Everyone is given *something* to do for Jesus!

Paul next describes God's plan for the paid clergy, as we would call them today. "And He Himself gave some to be apostles, some prophets, some evangelists, and some pastors and teachers" (Eph. 4:11, NKJV). What is to be their purpose? "For the equipping [notice this job description] of the saints [that's you and me] for the work of ministry, for the edifying of the body of Christ" (NKJV). In the next few verses Paul describes what a church with all members involved in ministry looks like: they have unity of faith; Christ is the head; they speak the truth in love; and they are growing.

I like the last phrase in verse 16—"growth of the body." That is God's plan for the men and women of the world: that they will accept Him (numerical growth), and that they will become like Him (spiritual growth). Our part is to accept the role in which God has called each of us to serve. It is as much a calling to be a lay member involved in ministry as it is to be paid clergy called to ministry. The church of God will not function according to God's will without both paid clergy and laity following faithfully their calling.

The Bible shares several methods of outreach that were used in the early Christian church. These methods are still valid, although changing cultures require that they be adapted. Before we review these, we must define our terms. Some people today do not like the term *laity* or *layperson,* since it tends to separate the nonclergy from the ordained clergy, even though the nonclergy are really ministers just like the ordained clergy. They prefer terms such as *minister, lay pastor, pastor,* or *volun-*

teer pastor. But because the terms *laity, laymen,* and *lay members* are easily understood and there is no exact substitute, these are the terms we will use in this book.

The Bible also uses sheep/shepherd terminology. A *pastor* (ordained) is a person commissioned to care spiritually for "lost sheep" as well as "found sheep." However, a survey of Scripture and Ellen White's comments would suggest that lost sheep should be their primary concern, including equipping the laity for ministry. The laity are generally viewed as the people of God in distinction from their ordained leaders. Scripture does make distinctions between leaders and members, but in the New Testament the *laos* (people of God) included both clergy and nonclergy. The modern word *laity* is used differently from the Greek word *laos*. For our purposes a layperson is not part of the ordained clergy and can be a church denominational employee.

Laymen in the New Testament "went everywhere preaching the word" (Acts 8:4, NKJV). Examples are Aquila, Priscilla, and Barnabas. The goal of the "going," according to Paul, was "that I might by all means save some" (1 Cor. 9:22, NKJV).

The New Testament does distinguish between evangelists and pastors, though it does not give a job description for these offices. It has been suggested that evangelists gave almost all of their time to winning "lost sheep." But the New Testament teaches that evangelism is the job of both ministers and church members. In addition, the paid clergy have the added responsibility to equip the members for ministry.[17]

New Testament Outreach Methods

Preaching. Paul said that with the "foolishness of preaching" some would be saved (1 Cor. 1:21). The foolishness is that God could proclaim the gospel without the aid of humankind; He has used donkeys and trumpets, and even the rocks could cry out if necessary. However, preaching is a primary means of gospel proclamation. The book of Acts bears this out.

Michael Green, in his book *Evangelism in the Early Church*, refers to three types of preaching—synagogue preaching, open air preaching, and prophetic preaching.[18] Preaching was an important factor among the methods of fulfilling the mission. Nevertheless, the "break with the synagogue, the rise of the persecution, and the absence of Christian buildings for worship all hindered formal proclamation of the gospel."[19]

It was not easy to gather a large group of people in the Roman Empire without inviting police action, and the major agents in the expansion of Christianity were men and women "who carried on their livelihood in some purely secular manner and spoke of their faith to those they met in this natural fashion."[20] Despite the difficulties, great numbers of Christians preached all over the world.

Ministry group. When Jesus wanted to impact the world, He began with a group of 12 men in whom He devoted His life, time, and energy. The 12 were a small group of men whom Jesus trained, equipped, and sent out to do ministry. We observe several small group principles at work among this ministry team.

Personal visitation. One method used effectively was sending out the disciples—usually in pairs—to visit people in their homes, public places, or the countryside. Examples of this in Scripture include Ananias's visit to Saul (Acts 9:10-18); Peter and John and the beggar in the Temple (Acts 3); Peter and the Roman officer (Acts 10); and Paul's conversation with the chief of the island after his shipwreck (Acts 28).

"In the work of disseminating the gospel," writes Ellen White, "Christ sent His disciples out by two and two. In our efforts we should follow the plan of our Master. There are many that think it would be more advantageous to scatter our forces as much as possible. . . . But Christ's way is best, and it will always result in loss to follow other methods than His."[21]

Teaching. Another method used throughout the New Testament and especially in the ministry of Jesus was teaching. The Gospels are filled with accounts of Jesus sitting down with a crowd, or discussing spiritual themes one-on-one. This was a method used effectively by the early church members.

Literature. The disciples soon realized that writing down Jesus' teachings and miracles would extend His influence to areas where they could not be available in person. Written information could be read many times, discussed, and passed on to others. John stated very openly the purpose of the literature: "These are written that you may believe that Jesus is the Christ, the Son of God, and that believing you may have life in His name" (John 20:31, NIV). John wanted to convince his readers that Jesus was the Messiah, the Son of God.

Testimony. As the early Christians shared the truth they found in Jesus, they also added their personal testimony. Justin Martyr used his testimony as a Christian convert very effectively in the second century. The Christians realized that no one could refute one's personal experience. As they shared and there was evidence of a changed life, it caused many to reflect upon their own life and personal needs.

Household evangelism. "One of the most important methods of spreading the gospel in antiquity was by the use of homes."[22] An example of how this method frustrated detractors of Christianity is seen in the words of a man named Celsus. He complained that the common people such as "wool workers, cobblers, laundry workers and yokels" were converted to Christianity in the homes of Christians. These home meetings consisted of any number of people from a handful to "considerable crowds."[23]

Synagogue evangelism. Christians seeking to share their faith went where the people were who were open to listening and talking about spiritual issues. They mingled with nonbelievers. This is a concept many Christians have overlooked today. It is both simple and profound—to catch fish you must go where the fish are. Acts 2:46 bears this out, stating that the believers went to the Temple and house-to-house.

Prayer. When the 12 disciples poured out their hearts to God in prayer, they were filled with the Holy Spirit, they spoke with boldness, and people believed and accepted Jesus. Paul knew that prayer was one of the ways to bind Satan and prepare people to hear the gospel. He asked the Ephesian church to pray for him so he could preach boldly. He asked the Corinthians to pray so the strongholds of evil could be broken. The apostles knew that God would not reveal Himself to nonbelievers unless they depended fully on God in prayer.

Church planting. One of the primary means of reaching the world was to start new churches. When a group of believers was established, a house church was begun. When one home filled up, another location was sought or a new church was begun. With an established base the Christians had a place to invite their friends and relatives to as they discussed their faith and worshiped.

The Adventist Merry-go-round

Ron Gladden and I like to refer to this variety of evangelistic methods as a merry-go-round. Why? Because evangelism is not an event, but a process; a way of life. It is an unending cycle of preparation, reaping, and follow-up. Even though there is a natural progression, contacts with non-Christians can occur at any time in this process. Because the process is cyclical, and people can get involved at any time, the evangelistic process is like a merry-go-round.

All parts of the process are necessary and biblical. Each method must work together with the others to accomplish the task of evangelizing the world. A successful small group strategy can use each of the previously mentioned methods effectively within the small group ministry.

That is why the Christian church has at various times in history grown numerically and spiritually using house evangelism as the primary method. The same thing can and should occur today. Here are the steps in the process:

Evangelistic Merry-Go-Round

1. Form friendships with neighbors, work associates, and casual contacts such as the store clerk, hairdresser, gas station attendant, etc.
2. Share your personal testimony about the benefits of Christianity.
3. Invite them to pathway events—health seminars, family issues, music programs, etc.
4. Invite them to worship services which display sensitivity to guests by being culturally relevant and demonstrating fellowship.
5. Invite them to reaping events such as crusades, seminars, house groups, classes.
6. Incorporate them into ministry teams (two by two) for visitation, literature distribution, community services, etc., where they can use their spiritual gifts.
7. Incorporate them into small groups of various types.
8. Disciple them so that they begin to spiritually reproduce by bringing others into the cycle.

As you can see, there are a variety of ways to share Jesus Christ. However, because this book is primarily about small groups—house evangelism—this will be our focal point. Other strategies are just as valid, but the small group method is the focus of this book. All of the above methods can be incorporated in a successful small group strategy.

The Poison of the Reformation

By now I am sure you have figured out that part of the poison that caused the Reformation still lingers in the Protestant church. It is a departure from God's plan to involve every member in active ministry. But there is hope. There are signs of a resurgent lay movement. There are reports from across North America of Adventist Church members involved in relational evangelism, establishing Bible correspondence schools, visiting door-to-door, participating in satellite reaping meetings, becoming Global Mission pioneers, and planting churches. There is also a strong prayer movement—a seeking of God in prayer for His Spirit. The refreshing rain is beginning to fall—the latter rain of the Holy Spirit.

I saw the rain of the Spirit in Harare, Zimbabwe. I was conducting a training seminar about how to use the small group as a process for nurturing newly baptized members, and as a continuing outreach method for those who had not made decisions for Jesus following an evangelistic reaping campaign. In my class was a man who had made a commitment to God to be involved in active ministry beginning January 1. Every day after work this man and his wife went door-to-door looking for individuals who wanted Bible studies. They had prayed and asked God to give them 50 Bible studies before April 1, when the evangelistic reaping meetings would begin. God heard their prayer and honored their faithfulness by giving them more than 50 people with whom to study. How excited they were! Twenty-five of those prospects were baptized during the meetings, and several others made decisions to be baptized. The man said he was very tired from all the work, but it was worth it. He was tremendously excited when he hit upon the idea of gathering those with whom he was studying into a small group. His eyes lit up as he realized that there was an alternative to individual Bible studies that also worked and would allow him to study with more than one family at a time.

The Spirit is falling around the world. Take courage! The bones are beginning to rattle—can you hear them?

---

[1] "Leaking Hanford Waste Demands Quick Action," Vancouver, Washington, *Columbian,* February 27, 1996.

[2] Phillip Schaff, *History of the Christian Church* (Grand Rapids: Eerdmans Pub. Co., 1959), vol. 1, p. 384.

[3] *Ibid.,* p. 379.

[4] *Ibid.,* p. 382.

[5] *Ibid.*

[6] *Ibid.*

[7] *Ibid.,* vol. 2, p. 46.

[8] *Ibid.,* p. 71.

[9] William Beckham, "The Two-winged Church Will Fly," *Seminar Notebook* (1996), p. 18.

[10] Russell Burrill, *Revolution in the Church* (Fallbrook, Calif.: Hart Research Center, 1993), p. 39.

[11] Ellen G. White, *Christian Service* (Takoma Park, Md.: General Conference of SDA, 1947), p. 10.

[12] C. Mervyn Maxwell, notes from Andrews University class lectures on SDA Church history; and Burrill, p. 41.

[13] E. G. White, *Testimonies,* vol. 7, p. 20.

[14] *Ibid.,* p. 19.

[15] *Ibid.,* p. 18.

[16] E. G. White, *Gospel Workers* (Washington, D.C.: Review and Herald Pub. Assn., 1915), p. 26.

[17] C. Mervyn Maxwell, notes from Andrews University class lectures on SDA Church history.

[18] Michael Green, *Evangelism in the Early Church* (Grand Rapids: William B. Eerdmans Pub. Co., 1970), pp. 194-200.
[19] *Ibid.,* pp. 202, 203.
[20] *Ibid.,* p. 203.
[21] E. G. White, in *Signs of the Times,* Jan. 23, 1893.
[22] Green, p. 207.
[23] *Ibid.,* p. 208.

Chapter Four

The Persecuted Church Model

The pastors sat before me with questioning looks on their faces. I was in the city of Vladivostok, Russia, conducting small group training and classes in pastoral leadership. They couldn't believe what they were hearing. Their response was "You mean that even though we have freedom to worship, we still need to meet in our homes for small group meetings?" The dilemma was that they had been secretly meeting in their homes for many years because of fear of the KGB, and the possibility of being sent to work camps in Siberia. Now that they had freedom, the Russian believers wanted to meet together publicly all the time!

I could understand their reasoning. The first time I shared a public worship service with our Russian members, I saw the joy and excitement on their faces. They never tired of fellowship, singing, Bible study, preaching, and sharing ideas. Some of their loved ones had died or suffered in prison for this privilege of worship.

A few days later, in fact, I was in the city of Novosibirsk, riding in the car with the conference president. He looked over at me and said, "God is so good! Fifty years ago there was a ministerial meeting just like the one you are conducting. One day in the middle of the meeting the KGB kicked in the door, arrested all 15 of the ministers, and sent them all to Siberia. One of them returned alive; the others died." I sat there stunned, wondering if I had the same kind of faith.

A few days later I was sitting beside a Bible worker. She pointed to a woman and said, "Her mother refused to give up the Sabbath." It turned out that the mother's punishment was that her daughter (the woman standing in front of me) was taken from her and never allowed to see her mother. No wonder freedom of worship meant so much to them!

What kept the church growing and vibrant during this time period of persecution? A key element was the home small group meetings—the house church. There was sharing, Bible study, prayer, worship, support and nurture, and outreach. Personal needs were met. Copies of the Bible and books by Ellen White were a rarity. I have seen complete copies of *The Desire of Ages* and parts of the Bible that were handwritten. They lived in fear of being arrested for their faith, but they also lived in peace in the arms of an understanding God.

We strongly encouraged our Russian brothers and sisters to continue meeting every Sabbath for public worship in their churches and meeting halls. We also suggested special meetings for the youth, vespers, training rallies, and any other type of public meeting they wished. But we urged them not to neglect the home small group. Together we analyzed the benefits of fellowship, support, interactive Bible study, and the outreach to nonbelievers that occurred in the groups. Once they saw the balance and understood what the Bible and Ellen White said about home group meetings, they were convinced. The Russian people eventually said that God had providentially led them in their system of home churches during the years of persecution.

Our team from the United States began calling the home small group system the persecuted church model, because it was so typical of the New Testament church and because this mode of worship has been most popular among Christians during times of persecution.

However, the home group strategy is more than simply a persecuted church model; it is a biblical approach that is a key ingredient of church life. Small group principles have been part of God's organizational plan for the church since the days of the Old Testament. Christianity is based on the concept of community—that is, relationships with God and with one another. A small group is where community is lived out at its best.

Small Groups in a Persecuted Church

During times of persecution the home small group concept flourishes and the church grows spiritually and numerically, but when the persecution is relaxed, there is a tendency to overlook small group life and become program-centered rather than group-centered.

In the 1970s missionaries from the Mennonite Church of America began to leave Ethiopia for permanent return to the United States, leaving an indigenous national church of 5,000 members. In 1982 the Communists overthrew the government of Ethiopia. The church began to suffer persecution. The Mennonites lost their church buildings and property; leaders were imprisoned; and members were forbidden to meet. The church went underground and became a home small group movement. Ten years later, in 1992, the Communist government was overthrown and the church came out of hiding. The Mennonites were surprised and rejoiced in the fact that the 5,000 members had grown to more than 50,000 members![1]

The second example involves a church that has flourished in a time of freedom by using the small group model. It is based in Seoul, South Korea. Once a 2,400-member traditional program-based church, it is now a small group-based church with more than 750,000 members. It changed because the pastor was on his sickbed and was forced to organize his church differently. Through Bible study, reflection, and prayer, God revealed to him a plan to empower the laity to ministry. The pastor called his deacons together and laid out the plan. The deacons agreed that the plan was biblical, but they all agreed that they were too busy to be part of it. The pastor then called his deaconesses together and gave them the same challenge. Two hundred women responded—10 percent of the membership—and began a small group movement. Today, through a ministry of prayer and small groups, the church has exploded across Korea.[2]

The early Adventist Church, like the New Testament church, followed a similar model of both public and house meetings. It is time that we reexamine our roots. Ellen White said, "We have nothing to fear for the future, except as we shall forget the way the Lord has led us, and His teaching in our past history."[3]

As Adventists we pray for, talk about, and look forward to the outpouring of the latter rain and a growth explosion of the church to take place in our lifetime. We firmly preach and believe it will take place prior to the second coming of Jesus. When this occurs, our traditional system will not be able to handle the growth! There will not be enough money to build church buildings. The church will grow so fast that our existing churches will not be able to handle the numbers, and eventually persecution will drive us away from the cities and our buildings. What is the solution? Scripture, Ellen White, and examples of recent past history in the Adventist Church have given us the answer: an empowered laity and home groups—a winning combination. We cannot ignore the Adventist Church experience in China.

The Adventist Church in China

In 1948 China was convulsed by civil war. City after city fell to the Communists, who swept down from the north. The war and the great floods left approximately 55 million Chinese homeless. Prices skyrocketed. Famine threatened. If anyone had an excuse to not worry about the preaching of the Word, it was the Chinese, who had to devote major amounts of time and energy to surviving.

However, sensing the shortness of the hour, Seventh-day Adventist missionaries and Chinese nationals launched Mission '48 on April 4, 1948, with 50 public meetings. The outreach, however, closed down very quickly. On December 9, 1948, a telegram was received by the General Conference: "Evacuating missionaries from north and central to south China." Early in 1949 the last American Adventist missionaries were evacuated.

Between 1949 and 1950 the official work of the church in China was slowly winding down. Beginning in 1951, Chinese SDA church leaders were being pressured by the Communists to close the work in China completely. By 1966 China's Red Guard had virtually wiped out what was left of the open Christian witness. Then came the silent years.[4]

In recent years, with great anticipation, Christians of all denominations wondered how Christianity fared during that period. Had Christianity been able to survive the expulsion of missionaries, the shutdown of churches, and harsh persecution? Not only had it survived, but membership had mushroomed![5] How was this possible? Home fellowship groups are the answer.

Christians in China had met in small informal home gatherings for worship, prayer, and Bible study. In this support setting they found faith, courage, strength, and hope to continue in the Christian faith.[6]

In 1976 the Chinese government began to relax its control in many areas, and the Christian work began to revive. Even though many Christian leaders were still in prison in 1977 and 1978, the house church movement accelerated.

Beginning in 1979 the government gradually permitted churches to reopen. In 1989 approximately 5,000 churches were open. Protestant church buildings accommodated 5 million each week, with numerous others meeting in homes.

In fact, some sources believe that at least 50 million Chinese attend house churches. In the rural areas of China the house church is flourishing rapidly. During the 1980s the Adventist Church grew from a few thousand to more than 70,000.[7] Since 1989 there has been a steady increase in baptisms. A key ingredient has been the combination of the small group (home meetings) and the large group meeting.

What is the small group ministry like in China? Recent communications reveal the following data. The groups meet in homes for a one- to two-hour meeting on various weeknights, depending upon the participants' schedules. Generally what occurs is an Adventist family shares their faith with a friend, relative, or neighbor. The person accepts the Adventist faith and joins the group. The group, along with the new Adventist Christian, invites the new person's family and friends to attend. Thus the group grows.

There are basically no pastors, so all groups are led by lay members, most of them women. They do most of the preaching, and they are the most powerful preachers. One of these women preachers has built up a church of 1,000 members and has personally baptized hundreds of converts! There is a comprehensive training program to develop group leaders, preachers, and other witnessing skills.

Records indicate that the smallest groups are about 16 people. When the group fills the house, they start a new group. In some cases the members will meet in the countryside under the trees and have a church service. At times up to 800 people have met in these situations. These larger meetings follow a format that is similar to a church service most of us have attended. In the home meeting it is a time of fellowship, prayer, and study. They usually study the Bible, sometimes another book.

I am told that those who attend the formal Adventist Church gatherings have a different outlook from those who attend the house groups. The church attendees simply attend and participate in a formal worship service and then go home and return the next week. Those who belong to the house groups are focused. They desire to come close to God, to learn to pray; they come for fellowship and encouragement, and they share experiences.

The Adventist Church is growing fastest in the poorer sections of China. The people focus on what God has to offer. They respond to the gospel very positively. The church develops slower in the larger cities. One individual summed it up this way: "There is a spirit of self-sacrifice among these house church groups that is hard to find in the more developed areas of China, or for that matter the rest of the world. There is a spirit of family, and a happiness that can't be found in society at large. These groups are generally evangelistic."

It is obvious that there is much we can learn from the experience of our Christian brothers and sisters in China. They are highly flexible, outreach-focused, dependent on God, and they evidence a passion for winning the lost to Jesus.

Using Old Methods in New Contexts

It is time to reexamine where we have been and where God wants us to go from here. We must blow the dust off of certain tried-and-true principles and begin to reimplement them, using contemporary methods. Ellen White put it this way: "Men are needed who pray to God for wisdom, and who, under the guidance of God, can put new life into the old methods of labor and can invent new plans and new methods of awakening the interest of church members and reaching the men and women of the world."[8]

It is obvious that if we want to finish the work on this earth, something has to change. It is interesting to me that Lyle Schaller, a highly respected author and church consultant in mainline Protestant churches, reflected Ellen White's sentiments when he said, "The old wineskins of denominations will not make it into the next millennium."[9] Schaller is referring to the lack of lay involvement in church ministry. The article continues, "Today equipping is more than a spiritual gifts seminar or a volunteer management program. It's not a program at all, but a whole paradigm shift in church leadership."[10]

In other words, no more business as usual. As Seventh-day Adventists we have had the counsel for many years that the consultants are now calling the "new wineskins" and "paradigm shift." They are saying that the lay leadership of the church will be actively involved in a team ministry that makes them producers and not spectator Christians. It is time for Seventh-day Adventists to move ahead by example and action. We have the counsel; why not take the lead?

Remember the balance of Ellen White:

"There must be no fixed rules; our work is a progressive work, and there must be room left for methods to be improved upon. But under the guidance of the Holy Spirit, unity must and will be preserved."[11]

"Means will be devised to reach hearts. Some of the methods used in this work will be different from the methods used in the work in the past; but let no one, because of this block, the way by criticism."[12]

A point that must be emphasized is that methods change, but standards and doctrines are not negotiable! As Seventh-day Adventists we have the unique message of the three angels of Revelation 14 to share with the inhabitants of the world. That's a nonnegotiable item. However, we must look continually for new and contemporary ways to share that message without compromise.

I am excited as I think about God's desire for your church and mine—an empowered lay movement using their ministry gifts in glorious harmony for the purpose of reaching unchurched people for Jesus.

---

[1] William Beckham, *The Second Reformation,* p. 29.

[2] *Ibid.*

[3] Ellen G. White, *Life Sketches of Ellen G. White* (Mountain View, Calif.: Pacific Press Pub. Assn., 1915), p. 196.

[4] Roland Hegstad, sermon on religious liberty, Oregon pastors' conference, January 1972.

[5] Roberta Hestenes, *Using the Bible in Groups* (Philadelphia: Westminster Press, 1983), p. 9.

[6] *Ibid.,* p. 10.

[7] *Adventist Review,* July 12, 1990.

[8] E. G. White, *Evangelism,* p. 105.

[9] Lyle Schaller, *Net Fax,* Apr. 1, 1996, p. 1, from *Current Thoughts and Trends,* June 1996, p. 3.

[10] Brad Smith, "Team Ministry in the 21st Century," p. 3.

[11] E. G. White, *Evangelism,* p. 105.

[12] *Ibid.*

Chapter Five

Why Cheryl Wasn't Missed

Her words still haunt me—"I didn't fit in"; "I'm not sure I belonged"; "People probably cared, but it just didn't work out." Those were the phrases Cheryl used to explain why after one year as a new Christian, she was no longer attending church. The reason had nothing to do with Bible doctrines, questions over the Sabbath, or pressure from relatives. It had everything to do with the need for belonging.

I can still remember the day I baptized Cheryl. She had attended an evangelistic reaping series and continued with Bible studies and attendance at church socials and worship. One of the "over 60 years of age" members of the church, Alice, took Cheryl, a 22-year-old, under her care. At every event Alice was there beside Cheryl, making sure she was not alone and introducing her to others. Eventually Cheryl was introduced to the young adults closer to her age. People were friendly, but close relationships never occurred. Cheryl was not invited to be part of anyone's life outside of the church meetings. Gradually she sensed she "didn't belong." It was several weeks before someone said, "Hey, where's Cheryl? I haven't seen her lately, have you?"

What Cheryl was looking for was relationships; community. The word *community* is usually associated with geography (neighborhood or city); sociology (natural birth family); political groups (the nation, state, county); or sometimes a support group (grief, divorce, addictions). Community is a group of people who have common goals in their personal lives, so they come together to form a supportive friendship with one another. The bottom line is that we need one another, and we need

God, in order to be physically, socially, mentally, and spiritually healthy.

God is community. The Father, Son, and Holy Spirit are one—there is unity, cooperation, teamwork, and a love for one another among the three members of the Godhead. It was because of their special relationship that they decided to express that love by creating others in their likeness to experience and enjoy the same relationship. During the creation of the world God said, "Let Us make man in Our image, according to Our likeness" (Gen. 1:26, NKJV). We read next that God says, "It is not good that man should be alone; I will make him a helper comparable to him" (Gen. 2:18, NKJV). We find community in relationships. God made men and women to have positive, supportive relationships with one another. It is unnatural to be out of harmony with God and one another. Whether married or single, we need each other, and we all need God.

Even non-Christians recognize the need for bonding with individuals who accept and love you just as you are. A few years ago one of the most popular television shows, *Cheers*, built its popularity upon this theme of relationships. At the beginning of every episode viewers were reminded that Cheers was a place where everybody knew your name. Unfortunately, this "place" was a tavern, but the need for community that it met is universal, and in some locations the church is falling down on the job. A friend of mine told me recently that a new Christian friend had been a bartender for 25 years. The former bartender told him that the tavern was friendlier than some churches he had attended.

Alone Against the World

Americans have a long tradition of individualism that stands in tension with the idea of community. We pride ourselves on our ability to take care of ourselves. We tell our kids as they are growing up: Stand on your own two feet. If you don't look out for yourself, no one else will. We hold up personal independence as a goal. But individualism has its disadvantages. Because of this spirit some have developed a "rights" mentality that takes priority over relationships. If the relationship is not "fulfilling"—whether it be marriage, children, friendship, job, church, etc.—they opt out. Decisions are made based not on what is best for society, their family, their church, etc., but what is best for "them."

If you are reading this book, you are probably not like this. With Christians selfishness takes a more subtle form. Sometimes those who participate in small groups attend only for what they can get out of it, and not in order to give as well as receive. In fact, *Newsweek* reported several years ago that there were some 15 million Americans in about 500,000 support groups in the United States. When asked why they belong to a group, many replied that the group provided someone to "listen to me." We should be glad that these individuals are attending groups, but for them to find healing and fulfillment there must be developed true community—finding a relationship with God and one another through both giving and receiving.[1]

This isolated elevation of the individual is a far cry from God's plan for individual uniqueness in the context of community. In the analogy of the church as a body, as seen in 1 Corinthians 12, every person has a unique role in the church. If one person suffers, the entire church community suffers. Each unique gift is needed and necessary.

It is in community that we are most challenged to grow up in Jesus. We do not lose our uniqueness in community—we find it. We are most uniquely ourselves when we are with others who need us to complement the mutual picture of God that we are creating. Together we become what we could not become alone. This is God's plan for His church.

The apostle Paul said it well in 2 Corinthians 5:15: "He died for all, that those who live should live no longer for themselves, but for Him who died for them and rose again." When one is connected to Jesus, self becomes secondary and others become primary. "Christianity builds no walls of separation between man and his fellow-man, but binds human beings to God and to one another."[2] Isn't this the goal of the church and Christianity—living in a unity and harmony that becomes an avenue for the outpouring of the latter rain of the Holy Spirit greater than what was seen at Pentecost?[3]

Recently I was conducting a training seminar on how to deal with conflict within small groups. After the meeting Jennifer, one of the group leaders, pointed to another small group leader, Sarah, and told me this story. When Sarah first began coming to the group, she had nothing positive to add to it; instead, she subtracted from it. Sarah was like a puppy that had been beaten. She would not look anyone in the eye; she sat with her head hanging down. Her comments were always negative. But the group praised her good qualities and made her feel accepted and needed. It wasn't long until she began to blossom. "Now look at her!" Jennifer exclaimed. Together we stood and watched a vivacious young woman laugh, smile, and hug her fellow group leaders. Sarah was now giving others what she had been given. She had received the Holy Spirit in a relationship with caring Christians.

I believe that one of the finest and most natural ways to create a caring church is through small groups. The remainder of this book will discuss how to make community a reality in your personal life and in your church through small group ministries.

---

[1] "Unite and Conquer," *Newsweek,* Feb. 5, 1990.

[2] Ellen G. White, *Gospel Workers,* p. 140.

[3] Julie A. Gorman, "Close Encounters—The Real Thing," *Christian Education Journal,* Vol. XIII, No. 3.

Chapter Six

A Biblical and Historical Perspective on Small Groups

As David Haney says, "The question Do you believe in small groups? is neither right nor wrong; it is late. It is like asking if one believes in rain or automobiles. Groups are! They are springing up spontaneously all over the world wherever God's movement is active and alert."[1]

A casual reading of Scripture informs the reader that small group and large group meetings have always been a part of spiritual life and biblical history. Numerous how-to books have been written on the subject, but still many Christians do not understand the biblical principles of small group ministry.

I believe part of the reason some have shied away from small group ministries is the "bad rap" small groups have taken over the past 40 years. In the 1950s small groups were seen as psychological therapy units. The 1960s brought the flower children, drugs, Jesus movement, and park and coffeehouse evangelism, out of which emerged sensitivity groups. The 1970s reaction held that privacy was important, and that spilling one's feelings to others was not healthy. All of this cast a shadow on the concept of small groups in some minds.

Because of this reaction, many Christians shied away from the biblical model of groups. There was a fear of damaging one's image by "wrong association." However, several Christian organizations attempted to put a positive spin on this dilemma. They tried to counteract Satan's counterfeit in an attempt to develop a positive small group model for the Christian church. These organizations made a significant contribution in moving the thinking of Christians toward a more positive and biblical model of small groups.

The Christian emphasis in the seventies and eighties was that groups were to build positive fellowship and bonding and unity among Christians. Songs were written that reflected this attitude, such as "We Are One in the Spirit." Fellowship and friendship were emphasized, with Bible study and prayer being secondary. Few regarded outreach to non-Christians as a significant part of group life. If an unbeliever attended the group, that was OK, but it wasn't encouraged. From an Adventist perspective, there were AYA groups for youth. A seminar ministry for adults was developed as an addition or alternative to evangelistic reaping meetings, and Revelation seminars were born. In addition, seminars on health topics and felt need issues sprang up almost overnight.

In the mid-eighties, as relational evangelism methods were being developed and small groups for outreach evangelism were exploding in other countries around the world, small groups began to emerge in Adventism. Interestingly, a North American Division survey of the witnessing methods used in 1990 by Seventh-day Adventists revealed that home fellowship groups were the number one method! The following chart reveals the top nine witnessing activities of that year. In fact, surveys reveal that some type of home meeting/small group and other relational evangelism activities are the preferred choice of most adults under 50 years of age.[2]

Participation in Witnessing Programs
North American Adventist Church Members

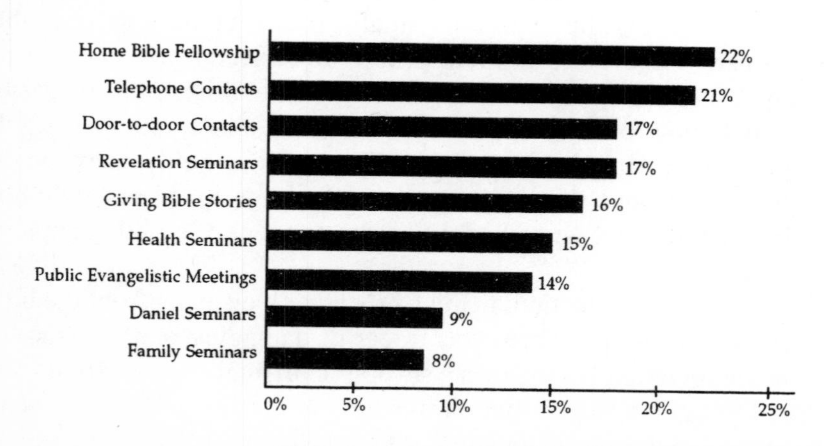

From the North American Division Church Information System Report 5 by Monte Sahlin.

As small groups began to gain a foothold in the Adventist Church, some criticism arose. Typical comments were: "Small groups are simply people sitting in a circle and pooling their ignorance"; or "A small group waters down the truth of Scripture"; or "I have never seen a decision for Jesus occur in a group—don't waste your time. Stick with public crusade evangelism." Part of the problem was that many people were basing their view of small groups on the outmoded practices of the fifties, sixties, and seventies, rather than on newer paradigms that were more scriptural. Also, change is difficult, but God's methods must and will adapt and change to a progressive environment. Society and culture never remain static, and we must move on.

Monte Sahlin, in his book *Sharing Our Faith With Friends*, has an excellent chapter on the history of evangelism in the Adventist Church. One section is especially useful for our purposes. Sahlin shares the concept that there have been three eras of evangelism in the Adventist Church. These are:

The Era of Prophetic Evangelism (1844-1900)

This period was characterized by an emphasis on the Word of God and a prophetic critique of the established churches. Targets included such social institutions as slavery, alcohol, dress, and diet. Preaching was the key method of this era. The camp meeting was instituted as a means of evangelism and as a key to revival in the Adventist member. The primary focus of evangelism was church planting. More than 1,500 local churches were organized during this time.[3]

The Era of Institutional Evangelism (1900-1980)

According to Howard B. Weeks, historian of Adventist evangelism, by the year 1900 tent meetings dealing with the topic of prophecy and Adventism were not as successful as they had been. The new era brought a focus on evangelistic preaching on the communication of a Christ-centered system of Adventist doctrine. Evangelistic lessons and standard topic outlines became a key part of the meetings. In this period the average congregation more than tripled in size from 36 members in 1900 to 110 members in 1963. In this era our hospitals, publishing houses, health food industry, and education system grew rapidly. The Adventist approach to ministry, like that of other denominations, was an assembly line approach. If a method worked, it was packaged and passed along to others. After all, why reinvent the wheel? Since we all have the same goal, many reasoned, let's use the same methods.[4]

The Era of Relational Evangelism (1980-Present)

During the eighties it became more and more difficult to get large numbers of pastors and congregations to cooperate in traditional institutionalized evangelism. A menu approach was developed. The new era appears to be characterized by an emphasis on sharing one's faith by meeting personal needs, establishing friendships, and then talking about Jesus and Bible doctrines. Fellowship is more important than organization and position and "climbing the ladder." The goal is to meet the needs of people rather than to build up institutional programs. Various methods of previous eras are merged with some newer methods. Home fellowship groups/small groups have emerged as one of the leading strategies of this era.[5]

This historical movement in the Adventist Church in the past few years is a reflection of contemporary society. Large bureaucratic institutions are downsizing. Top-down-controlled systems are giving way to decentralized democratic networks called quality-control circles. A new paradigm is emerging in which work is accomplished through partnerships, networking of colleagues and coworkers. People are viewed as more important than productivity. It is believed that if people feel they belong, then productivity will increase. "We have moved from the pyramid to the circle, from power down to power around, from bureaucracy to organic structures that enable a group to serve one another as well as the world."[6]

Some today are saying that the interest in and need for small group process is a new paradigm shift. However, Christians simply have to look at Christian history and Scripture to realize that this is not the case. Small groups are reflective of God's original intent for His church. Let's look together at the supporting evidence, keeping in mind that we are looking at principles. The application of these principles will vary with culture and circumstance.

Old Testament Principles

The principles of small group ministries can be traced to the first verse in the Old Testament, Genesis 1:1: "In the beginning God created the heavens and the earth" (NKJV). The word for God in the original language is plural, which includes more than one Person involved in Creation. Christian belief holds that the members of the Godhead—the

Father, Son, and Holy Spirit—are one in purpose and design—a small group, if you please.

After the human race was created in the image and likeness of God (Gen. 1:27), God said something that provides us with something of a rationale for small groups: "It is not good for the man to be alone" (Gen. 2:18, NIV). Men and women were created as social creatures; they live happier and more productive lives in groups. The family unit was given to fulfill basic human needs. Just as a newborn baby needs the love and attention of a family for healthy development, so a newborn child of God needs the nurture that only a small attentive group from the larger church family can give them. Genesis 2:18 does not mean that everyone has to be married to find fulfillment in life, but it does imply that as humans we need each other socially.

When God in Eden created the first man and woman, He formed a small community in relationship to Himself. They walked together "in the cool of the day" (Gen. 3:8). Next God gave them a task to do together with Him: they were to tend the garden (Gen. 2:15). They were also told to be fruitful and multiply (Gen. 1:28), increasing the size of their group.

We see here several key principles of group life. A small group is a minimum of three individuals—two humans and God. They interact and do things together. They desire for others to join their group and add to their social and spiritual development.

Adam and Eve being the first created couple also formed a household and gave birth to all people and nations that followed. Because of sin, God's plan of community and harmony was periodically disrupted, as for example in the dispute between Cain and Abel, and at the Tower of Babel. But God proposed to bring restoration to these fractured relationships. Abraham and his household group were brought into the covenant. The kingdom was promised to David and his household. The plan involved the Israelites as the nation God would use as His example to accomplish this task.

God's organizational structure for Israel involved large, medium, and small group relationships. The nation was composed of groups and subgroups of various sizes: it was divided into tribes, which were divided into clans, which were divided into families and individual households. In the same manner spiritual Israel, God's church today, needs to have competent and balanced leadership on each level of the organizational structure. If the church overlooks any of these groupings, it will suffer in its mission.

The Old Testament concept of organizing from large to small is also seen in the leadership advice that Jethro, Moses' father-in-law, gave to him while the Israelites were wandering in the desert. Pastor Moses had a church membership of more than 2 million. Exodus 38:26 states that the church in the wilderness was comprised of 603,550 men. Adding a wife and several children to each couple makes for a large congregation! It was no wonder Moses "pulled his pastoral hair" and said, "How can I alone bear your problems and your burdens and your complaints?" (Deut. 1:12, NKJV). It is obvious that the task facing Moses was impossible. Many pastors today attempt to minister to a congregation with very little assistance. It is impossible for pastors to meet the needs of all their members alone. That is one reason it is important for all members to assist in ministry.

Jethro (Ex. 18:21-23) told Moses to select able men who feared God, men of truth who were not greedy, and place them over the people. He instructed Moses to divide the people into groups of thousands, hundreds, fifties, and tens. This would mean that Moses needed in approximate round numbers 60,000 leaders of 10, 12,000 leaders of 50, 6,000 leaders of 100, and 600 leaders of 1,000, for a total of 78,600 leaders. Selecting the leaders and writing job descriptions for each must have been quite a task in itself. But God inspired Moses to follow these orders explicitly.

Sometimes pastors and lay leaders say it is not practical, necessary, or possible to organize a church into small groups. But Moses did! His smallest group was a unit of 10 people with a leader—the subject of this book!

Think about what occurred when Moses, and later Joshua, followed God's organizational structure—it led them to the Promised Land of Canaan. This was good, but God wanted them to completely occupy the land. Unfortunately, the Israelites quit before their mission was accomplished. They became complacent and didn't complete the task of winning Canaan completely for God.

Sometimes churches today do the same. Once they establish themselves in a community and attain a certain size, the members become complacent. They grumble that they are large enough already; if they get too big they will become impersonal. And they have many other excuses. But the mission of the church is not accomplished until Jesus returns. Jesus said to go into all the world, to every race, tribe, and people. It is not enough simply to be present in a community; we must "occupy." We must organize the church for service. And group ministry is a part of God's plan.

Jesus and Small Groups

When Jesus was ready to found the Christian church, He began with a small group. Matthew 4:18-22 and Luke 6:13-16 list the 12 disciples Jesus chose. They needed some rough edges of character sanded off, but they were the beginnings of Christianity.

The number 12 is interesting. Sociologists tell us that once a group becomes larger than 12, the dynamic changes and it is no longer a small group but a midsize group. That is why it is important for a small group to divide once it reaches approximately 12 members. If it doesn't, the survival rate is not good, because the small group dynamic is no longer present. However, some groups manage this issue by meeting as a larger group, and then dividing into smaller units that meet throughout the house for discussion and interaction.

Another interesting small group phenomenon occurred within the 12 disciples. Jesus and the other disciples had close friends among themselves. Jesus had a special closeness to Peter, James, and John. In the Garden of Gethsemane (Matt. 26) Jesus asked the three to pray with Him, while the others were left in another part of the garden. Likewise on the Mount of Transfiguration (Matt. 17:1-3). There is nothing wrong with group members bonding with one another; this is quite natural. Encouraging close friendships and prayer partnerships among the various members will assist the group members in ministering to one another and will strengthen your group. In addition, when it is time for your group to divide, encourage the group to divide according to their special relationships, and it will be easier for the group.

Which is more important, small group or large group time? The answer is that small groups and large groups should not compete. The church needs both. This is especially true in evangelism, when small groups and reaping crusades are combined to provide nurture and reaping. When the newly baptized and those still seeking Jesus are placed in groups, there is a weekly accountability and ready-made family to assist in the spiritual growth of the individual. Jesus spent time with the multitudes, time with the individual, and time in homes. He visited the home of Simon the leper; He spent time with the woman at the well; He had an encounter with Zacchaeus. Scripture says that when He saw the multitudes, He was moved with compassion for them. Small group and large group time is like faith and works—the two cannot be separated.

Jesus spent time with His small group, the disciples. He bonded with them, instructed them, prayed with them, and then took them with Him to observe Him ministering to others. Afterward they retreated into their small group and debriefed and processed their ministry and mission (Matt. 14:13-23; Mark 3:7). A casual reading of the Gospels reveals that Jesus spent more time one-on-one or in small group settings than in large group settings. Why? Because people are saved as individuals, not as a multitude.

Jesus always put people before structure and traditions. His goal was redemptive relationships. He told the disciples if someone wants to be a leader in His organization, they must put others before themselves. One must be willing to serve others and give up selfish goals and desires (Luke 22:24-30). In addition Jesus told the religious leaders that their priority should be living the principles of the kingdom and not policing the rules of the kingdom. He said it's what's on the inside of the person that counts, not the outward appearance (Luke 17:20, 21). Once the relationship is correct, obedience will follow. In everything the church does, including small groups, people must be the number one priority. Members should not participate in group life to "fix" one another. It is the role of the Holy Spirit to convict and change lives. The members are to learn and live Scripture and support and pray for one another.

Jesus also used the small group setting with His disciples to train them for service. It was a safe environment to share concerns and questions and be able to grow from the experience. An example is the parable of the sower in Luke 8. The disciples were sitting with the crowd listening to Jesus share the story and its application to life and ministry. When the disciples were alone with Jesus, they asked Him to explain the parable to them. I am sure the discussion assisted in their understanding the practics of soul winning. Similarly, the small group environment provides opportunity for each member to minister to the others in the group, invite their friends and relatives, and learn ministry in a nonthreatening setting.

Jesus used the small group setting not only for sharing spiritual lessons, but as an environment in which to model leadership. The disciples were jealous of one another and fought with each other about who would be first in the kingdom. He was able to explain to them that the gifts of each person were to work in harmony with those of others under the guidance of the Holy Spirit (Luke 22:24-30; Matt. 18:1-5).[7]

Home-based small groups were important to Jesus in the formation, development, and success of the Christian church. Often His ministry occurred in the context of a home: "Then Jesus . . . went into the house. And His disciples came to Him" (Matt. 13:36, NKJV). And while in the house He taught them. "He went into the Pharisee's house and sat down to eat"

(Luke 7:36, NKJV); then He proceeded to teach Simon about forgiveness. In short, Jesus began the Christian church and His ministry to the world through a small group. His example should speak volumes to His church today. It is time we went back to the original design—it is time for small groups!

The Early Christian Church and Small Groups

The early believers called the church a "household of faith" (Gal. 6:10). Paul offered encouragement to the young members by continually reminding them they belonged to a spiritual family. They were members of "the household of God" (Eph. 2:19). Peter used the same metaphor and expanded the concept to mean the members were a "spiritual house" (1 Peter 2:5) in which God lived.

This metaphor edged over into reality, because in the first century Christian life centered around private homes. Christians were not allowed to build church buildings until after A.D. 313. The home became the meeting place of the early believers. Four examples are the church in the house of Mary, the mother of John Mark (Acts 12:12), the church in the house of Priscilla and Aquila (Rom. 16:3-5; 1 Cor. 16:19), the church in the house of Philemon (Philemon 2), and the church in the house of Nympha (Col. 4:15). Acts 2:41-47 indicates that the early Christian community was a tightly knit community that shared their resources and met daily for Bible study, fellowship, prayer, and praise.

Clement, one of the early church fathers, describes a house meeting that he visited: "The master of the house welcomed us, and led us to a certain apartment, arranged like a theater, and beautifully built. There we found considerable crowds waiting for us, who had come during the night."[8]

There were a variety of types of house meetings. The book of Acts reveals the following types:

- Prayer meeting (Acts 12:12)
- Evening of Christian fellowship (Acts 21:7)
- Common meals, possibly Communion services (Acts 2:46)
- A night of prayer, worship, and instruction (Acts 20:7)
- Impromptu evangelistic gatherings (Acts 16:32)
- Planned meetings to present the gospel (Acts 10:22)
- Following up of those inquiring about the gospel (Acts 18:26)
- For organizational instruction (Acts 5:42)

There was balance between the home and public meetings and a "winning combination" in the nurture and evangelistic methods that were followed. After the outpouring of the Holy Spirit, Scripture states the believers met daily "in the temple courts and from house to house," teaching about Jesus (Acts 5:42, NIV). Later we see Paul doing the same. He also taught and evangelized "from house to house" (Acts 20:20, NIV). Meetings in the homes provided the backbone of the church structure. However, the homes were not the only context in which the church functioned.

Large mass meetings were also part of the evangelistic strategy, such as meetings in the Temple and in synagogues. An example of this is the preaching of Peter in Acts 2, when 3,000 believers were added to the church.

The synagogues were the "church buildings" for the Jews. At first Christians met with them, not considering themselves a separate denomination, but only a reformed group within Judaism. But as Christians continued preaching and teaching, opposition followed from the Jewish leaders. Eventually Christians were barred from the synagogues and were forced to meet in private homes, where neighbors could be invited to discuss and listen to the gospel story with less danger of being interrupted.

However, except at certain periods of intense persecution, Christians were able to witness in the marketplace. An excellent modern-day example of marketplace evangelism was shared with me by one of our Russian leaders. During the height of the persecution of Christians in Russia, public and private meetings of Christians were banned, especially any evangelizing. The believers worked around this as best they could. One way was to go to the open market every week.

One of our pastors took a rooster with him every week and stood in the market with it. Other Adventist Church members would stand and talk with him, pretending they were discussing the purchase of the rooster. In reality they were discussing the Sabbath school lesson, church business, evangelism, or sometimes giving a Bible study. Sometimes a member would also bring something to sell to the market and would stand by the pastor with the rooster. Staring straight ahead, they would discuss church and spiritual issues. One day a KGB officer approached our pastor and said, "What is wrong with your rooster? You have brought him to the market for weeks. Many people talk to you about it and look it over, but no one buys it!" Through these and other risky methods the church grew and prospered in Russia.

The early church members must have used similar strategies in times of persecution. Persecution cannot quench the gospel. As one of the church fathers stated, "the blood of Christians is seed."

By the time of the Roman emperor Nero, Christians began to draw attention as a separate group from Judaism. In A.D. 64, 33 years after the death of Jesus, Nero declared that Christians and other specified "sects" could not build churches or other public meeting places.[9] Violators who attempted to worship Jesus publicly could possibly lose their property, Roman citizenship, and in some cases their lives.

We have already seen how Nero and Trajan repressed Christianity by banning public assembly. There is but one historical reference to a building for Christian gatherings prior to A.D. 300, and that was in Persia in A.D. 265, outside the Roman Empire.[10]

The strength of the Christian home church during this time was illustrated by an incident in A.D. 170. The Roman emperor issued a decree that Christians in Alexandria were to "desist from their faith and meetings" or Roman armies would be sent to destroy them. The bishop of Alexandria (the largest city in Egypt at that time) responded by stating that in order to destroy the Christians, more than half the city's population would have to be executed.[11]

In the fourth century the emperor Constantine declared Christianity the official religion of the Roman Empire. This decree resulted in church building projects throughout the empire. With religion and government headquarters in Rome, church and state leaders joined hands to promote the growth of Christianity.

The steps leading to Constantine's decree began in A.D. 311 in the city of Nicomedia by the Roman emperor Galerius. Galerius declared "that the purpose of reclaiming the Christians from their willful innovation and the multitude of their sects to the laws and the discipline of Roman state was not accomplished; and that he would now grant them permission to hold their religious assemblies, provided they disturbed not the order of the state."[12]

Constantine's decree in A.D. 313 went beyond Galerius' decree. It was a decisive step from hostile neutrality to friendly neutrality and protection. It prepared the way for Christianity to be the legally recognized religion of the Roman Empire. The decree ordered the immediate, full restoration of all confiscated church property at the expense of the Roman treasury.[13]

Constantine, following his decree, led the way in building church structures with elaborate architecture. He immediately built magnificent churches in Jerusalem, Bethlehem, and Constantinople.

Eusebius, an early church historian, describes a church built in Tyre between A.D. 313 and 322. He states it included a large porch, a quadrangular atrium surrounded by columns, a fountain in the center of the atrium for those attending to wash their hands and feet before entering, interior porticoes, galleries, altars, thrones for the bishops, and benches for the church members. Building materials included cedar of Lebanon, granite, and other precious materials.[14]

Church: Building or Body?

Church/state alliances and institutionalism had a negative effect upon the church. The ensuing period is known today as the Dark Ages. During this time the church's spiritual fellowship and sense of community were to some degree exchanged for buildings, ritual, and formality. The house meeting was virtually lost as the medium of spiritual life. The "church" came to mean a building—bricks and mortar.

Instead of attending church in their homes, the Christians met in the church building for their weekly worship. In place of the weekly home meeting led by the laity, the members now attended a midweek service in the church building led by the priest. The role of the paid clergy changed from equippers, evangelists, overseers, and church planters to worship leaders and preachers. The role of the laity changed from witnesses to spectators and assistants of the paid clergy.

In addition, the church building replaced the home as the center of church life. I am not implying that public places of worship are wrong. We have already stated that the Christian church must have both home small groups and public meetings. But the church lost its balance. Bill Beckham refers to this balance by the metaphor of "the two-winged church."[15] He says just as an airplane or bird cannot fly with one wing, so the church cannot accomplish its task imbalanced in its approach.

As a boy I would purchase balsa-wood gliders and throw them into the air. If the glider was not assembled correctly and the wings were not properly attached, the plane would either go around in circles or crash to the ground. Likewise, if the church is not balanced in its nurture and evangelism, the world will not be given the gospel message as commissioned by Jesus.

A Spirit-filled Approach

My church members have asked me, "Pastor, what does a Spirit-filled church look like? How is it supposed to function? What methods will it use?" To answer that question, I usually direct them to the second chapter of Acts in the Bible. This chapter is must reading for an understanding of Spirit-filled church life.

A summary of the background of Acts 2 is as follows:

- Jesus told the disciples He was going to return to heaven (John 13:33).
- Jesus told the disciples that He would not leave them alone, but would give them the Holy Spirit (John 14:15-18).
- Jesus told the disciples that the Holy Spirit would be their helper. He would teach them and help them remember what Jesus taught them (John 14:26).
- Jesus assured the disciples it was to their advantage that He return to heaven. The Holy Spirit, whom Jesus would send, would convict the world of sin, of right living, and about the need to make a decision for Jesus (John 16:7-15).
- After His resurrection, just before He returned to heaven, Jesus gave the disciples what Christians call the Great Commission. He told all Christians to go and make disciples, baptize, and teach in all nations (Matt. 28:18-20).
- Jesus then told the disciples to wait in Jerusalem for the Holy Spirit to come upon them (Acts 1:4).
- Jesus told the disciples that they would receive power and be His witnesses all over the world when the power of the Holy Spirit came upon them (Acts 1:8).

Acts 2 describes the disciples receiving the power of the Holy Spirit. What follows the first four verses is a description of what a Spirit-filled church looks like. In verses 22-36 Peter preaches to the people about the fact that Jesus is the Messiah, the Saviour of the world, and the Son of God. After hearing the sermon, the people cried, "What shall we do?" (verse 37). He told them to repent and be baptized for the forgiveness of sins, and 3,000 people responded to the call and were baptized (verses 38-41).

What follows the baptism is a description of what church life was like for these newly baptized members of the newly formed, relatively pristine, Spirit-filled church. Verse 42 describes four items that were part of their daily life. *First*, the believers devoted themselves to the apostles teachings. Today we would call this Bible study. *Second*, there was fellowship—love, caring, sharing, nurture—with one another. *Third*, they broke bread together. They shared a common meal daily. *Fourth*, they prayed together.

Verse 43 adds a *fifth* element. It says there were miracles and signs that occurred in the church. Other Bible references mention conversions, healings, and even resurrections.

Verses 44 and 45 add a *sixth* dimension. They state that the believers had "all things in common" and gave of their physical possessions to anyone who had need. Some believers had lost their possessions when they became Christians. New Christians sometimes found themselves without a job, money, or a home. Thus the members of the church assisted one another and met the personal needs of its members. Today those needs might include financial help with food, housing, utilities, or medical bills. In addition it might include alcohol and drug rehabilitation and recovery from other addictive habits.

Verse 45 states that the members met in the "temple" (mass meeting) and "house to house" (small home meeting and one-on-one friendship evangelism), and "the Lord added to the church daily those who were being saved" (verse 47, NKJV). The mass meetings and home meetings not only provided support, fellowship, and social life, but soul winning occurred—people were baptized. Some say that the purpose of small groups is to meet social needs. That is true—but the biblical model also produces decisions for Jesus Christ! *If your small group does not have outreach as part of its format, then your group is not following the God-given model found in Acts 2.*

A friend of mine visited a small group. Members were studying Bible prophecy and had Christians and seekers (people who haven't accepted Jesus) attending. During the meeting it was obvious that Martha, one of the non-Christians, did not understand the Bible study. At the end of the meeting my friend was talking with Martha. She told him that she was going to become a Christian and join the Seventh-day Adventist Church. He was curious, because he knew she did not understand the prophecy in Daniel 9 that the group had just studied. My friend questioned Martha about her understanding of the teachings of the Adventist Church. She responded, "There are some things I don't understand. But those that I do understand I know are true. Once I continue to study and understand that which is not clear to me, I know I will find it biblical, because everything I have understood so far is rooted in Scripture. Besides, these people love me; they are my family."

This is what small groups are all about!

---

[1] Miquel Cerna, *The Power of Small Groups in the Church* (Newbury Park, Calif.: El Camino Pub., 1991), p. 15.

[2] "Church Members: Involvement, Witnessing, Devotions." North American Division Information System, Report Five (Silver Spring, Md.: North American Division of SDA, 1991), p. 8.

[3] Monte Sahlin, *Sharing Our Faith* (Hagerstown, Md.: Review and Herald Pub. Assn.), pp. 14, 15.

[4] *Ibid.,* pp. 15-18.

[5] *Ibid.,* pp. 20-23.

[6] Gareth Weldon Icenogle, *Biblical Foundations for Small Group Ministry* (Downers Grove, Ill.: InterVarsity Press, 1994), pp. 9-12.

[7] Neal F. McBride, *How to Lead Small Groups* (Colorado Springs, Colo.: NavPress, 1990), pp. 15-18.

[8] Michael Green, *Evangelism in the Early Church,* p. 208.

[9] Phillip Schaff, *History of the Christian Church,* vol. 1, p. 384.

[10] Albert J. Wollen, *Miracles Happen in Group Bible Study* (Glendale, Calif.: 1976), p. 30.

[11] *Ibid.,* p. 29.

[12] Schaff, vol. 2, p. 71.

[13] *Ibid.,* p. 72.

[14] *Ibid.,* pp. 198-202.

[15] William Beckham, *The Two-winged Church Will Fly.*

Chapter Seven

The Adventist Church and Small Groups

The Seventh-day Adventist Church grew out of the Millerite movement of the 1840s, which drew adherents from several mainline denominations. One of these was the Methodist Church. Ellen White was baptized into the Methodist Church in 1842. She described the event in these words. "It was a windy day when we, twelve in number, went down into the sea to be baptized. The waves ran high and dashed upon the shore, but as I took up this heavy cross, my peace was like a river. When I arose from the water, my strength was nearly gone, for the power of the Lord rested upon me. I felt that henceforth I was not of this world, but had risen from the watery grave into a newness of life. The same day in the afternoon I was received into the church in full membership."[1]

As a member in the Methodist Church, Ellen White became involved in what were called "class meetings."[2] This practice originated in England, and later developed into our weekly prayer meeting. In order to understand this, we must go back to England in the nineteenth century and review the ministry of John Wesley, the founder of the Methodist Church.

In the years following the Reformation, Christianity continued to enjoy popular acceptance, but church institutional formality returned. Because of this, home group meetings withered, and the influence of Christianity declined in the early eighteenth century in the face of the European Industrial Revolution. But John Wesley and George Whitefield were used by God to spearhead a spiritual revival in England.

Wesley and Whitefield traveled the English countryside, calling people back to God. As individuals made decisions for Christ, they were organized into societies. These societies met together in rented facilities for prayer, Bible study, fellowship, and worship.[3]

In Bristol, England, a problem arose in various societies concerning how to raise the money to pay their monthly rent for public meeting places. Consequently, Wesley divided the societies into groups of 12 individuals. He assigned a leader in each group to collect a penny weekly from each family to pay the rent. As the leaders collected the pennies, they reported back to Wesley that they discovered drinking problems, marriage difficulties, and other situations that shouldn't be a part of the Christian lifestyle.

After this revelation the collection plan was revised. The 12 group members began to meet in one of the members' houses, and they began to discuss openly their personal problems for mutual edification.[4]

The spiritual and personal growth in the lives of the society group members was phenomenal. Word of the positive influence of the Bristol societies traveled to London. Within a short time the London society divided into groups of 12. Out of this simple beginning came the Methodist class meetings. These groups provided Bible study, prayer, testimonies, and fellowship. It was from this group process that the Wesleyan revival in England flourished. It was a revival led by lay members, not paid clergy—lay members opening the Bible in homes all across England.

Wesley's movement (called Methodist because they followed specific methods to accomplish ministry) eventually jumped the Atlantic. Churches were built, and public meetings combined with the small class meetings provided the basis for the growth of Methodism in the United States.[5]

The small group movement in Methodism also had an impact on the Seventh-day Adventist Church because of the influence of Ellen White. In her youth she became involved in the Millerite movement and the subsequent formation of the Seventh-day Adventist Church. Early in her experience Ellen White recognized the positive spiritual benefits of small group ministry. Consequently she penned the following statements under the direction of God:

"Preach less, and educate more, by holding Bible-readings, and by praying with families and little companies. To all who are working with Christ I would say, Wherever you can gain access to the people by the fireside, improve your opportunity. Take your Bible, and open before them its great truths. Your success will not depend so much upon your knowledge and accomplishments, as upon your ability to find your way to the heart. By being social and coming close to the people, you may turn the current of their thoughts more readily than by the most able discourse. The presentation of Christ in the family, by the fireside, and in small gatherings in private houses, is often more successful in winning souls to Jesus than are sermons delivered in the open air, to the moving throng, or even in halls or churches."[6]

"Let small companies assemble together in the evening or early morning to study the Bible for themselves. Let them have a season of prayer that they may be strengthened and enlightened and sanctified by the Holy Spirit. . . . If you will do this, a great blessing will come to you from the One who gave His whole life to service, the One who redeemed you by His own life. . . . What testimonies you should bear of the loving acquaintance you have made with your fellow workers in these precious seasons when seeking the blessing of God. Let each tell his experience in simple words. . . . Let little companies meet together to study the Scriptures. You will lose nothing by this, but will gain much."[7]

Ellen White had another opportunity to observe the impact of small groups upon a country and a city. From 1891 to 1900 Ellen White was in Australia assisting with the development of the Seventh-day Adventist Church. While in Australia she assisted in the establishment of Avondale College and wrote several books, such as *The Desire of Ages* and *Steps to Christ.*

I believe God placed Ellen White in Australia for another significant reason. Ellen White had already experienced firsthand the power of small groups. Now God was placing her in a country where a small group revival was taking place. This would also provide an opportunity to reinforce the spiritual power of small group ministries in the mind and experience of Ellen White.

During the 1890s in Australia, the time of Ellen White's ministry there, events took place that were related to what is known today as the Welsh Revival. The clergy in and around Melbourne met together to pray for the spiritual health of their members and compatriots. The pastors gained so much strength from this time together that they believed the best thing they could do for their members' well-being was to organize them into similar groups for Bible study, prayer, and fellowship. Consequently, in the city of Melbourne 2,000 home meetings were occurring weekly at the peak of the revival.

The Melbourne pastors involved in small group ministry invited

R. A. Torrey to come from America and conduct an evangelistic campaign. The result was a tremendous revival.

A young woman was visiting Melbourne at this time from Wales. Taking her spiritual experience back to Wales, she assisted in the cottage prayer meetings of Wales. The cottage meeting contributed to the Welsh Revival, which had a tremendous impact on the development and growth of Christianity in Wales.[8]

During this same time period that impacted the Christian church in Australia, God emphasized to Ellen White the importance of small group ministry:

"The formation of small companies as a basis of Christian effort is a plan that has been presented before me by One who cannot err. If there is a large number in the church, let the members be formed into small companies, to work not only for the church members but for unbelievers also."[9]

"But on such occasions as our annual camp meetings we must never lose sight of the opportunities afforded for teaching the believers how to do practical missionary work in the place where they may live. In many instances it would be well to set apart certain men to carry the burden of different lines of educational work at these meetings. Let some help the people to learn how to give Bible readings and to conduct cottage meetings. Let others bear the burden of teaching the people how to practice the principles of health and temperance, and how to give treatments to the sick. Still others may labor in the interests of our periodical and book work."[10]

"Let the teachers in our schools devote Sunday to missionary effort. Let them take the students with them to hold meetings for those who know not the truth. Sunday can be used for carrying forward various lines of work that will accomplish much for the Lord. On this day house-to-house work can be done. Open-air meetings and cottage meetings can be held."[11]

As can be seen through history and the pen of Ellen White, God has eternal purposes in mind through small groups. As God revealed events to occur preceding the second coming of Jesus, small groups and sharing the Scriptures with neighbors are an important part of God's plan. The following comments are very convincing:

"In visions of the night, representations passed before me of a great reformatory movement among God's people. Many were praising God. The sick were healed, and other miracles were wrought. A spirit of intercession was seen, even as was manifested before the great Day of Pentecost. Hundreds and thousands were seen visiting families and opening before them the Word of God. Hearts were convicted by the power of the Holy Spirit, and a spirit of genuine conversion was manifest. On every side doors were thrown open to the proclamation of the truth. The world seemed to be lightened with the heavenly influence. Great blessings were received by the true and humble people of God. I heard voices of thanksgiving and praise, and there seemed to be a reformation such as we witnessed in 1844."[12]

"I saw the saints leaving the cities and villages, and associating together in companies, and living in the most solitary places. Angels provided them food and water, while the wicked were suffering from hunger and thirst."[13]

Ellen White uses terms such as *cottage meeting, small companies, little companies*, and *small gatherings* to refer to what we call small groups. Consider the elements of her counsel:

1. God told her that large churches should have small groups.
2. Small groups commonly meet in "private houses."
3. Meet by the "fireside."
4. Meet in the evening or morning, whichever is convenient for one's schedule.
5. The purpose of the meeting is to minister to baptized "church members"; for "winning souls to Jesus"; to minister to "unbelievers."
6. What is done during the meeting? (a) "open your Bibles," "study the Bible," "present Christ," "Bible readings"; (b) pray; (c) "be social," "come close to the people," "find your way to the heart"; (d) "share testimonies."

Ellen White's comments concerning small group life reflect very closely the elements of Acts 2:42-47: doctrinal study, home fellowship, prayer, food, and outreach.

Types of Adventist Meetings

Ellen White used several terms in describing various types of meetings in the Adventist Church. The terminology and practice has varied somewhat over the years, but the principles remain.

1. *Cottage Meeting:* This was a small group meeting during the week for Bible study, prayer, fellowship, and sharing of testimonies. The emphasis was on Bible study. The group usually met in private homes. The groups followed a format in their meetings that reached out to both church members and unbelievers. The terms *little companies* and *small companies* appear to refer to these cottage meetings.

2. *Bible Readings:* C. Mervyn Maxwell, Adventist Church historian, states that the first Bible reading in the Adventist Church occurred as the

result of a storm during a camp meeting in California. When the noise of the storm made preaching impractical, someone picked up a Bible and began asking questions along a doctrinal theme, inviting the congregation to look up the texts that answered the questions. This simple question-and-answer method caught on and became quite popular. Eventually a call went out for people to send in their favorite Bible readings. The best of these were compiled in 1888 into the first edition of the book *Bible Readings for the Home Circle.*

Evidently the Bible reading was similar to what we would call today a seminar or workshop. At times Ellen White refers to church members giving Bible readings and meeting in small companies as if they are two different meetings. At other times it would appear as if the two meetings could be held simultaneously. Evidently the home could be used not only for small group meetings, but for a Bible lecture series similar to the seminars conducted today, such as Revelation or Daniel seminars, Discover Jesus seminars, etc.

In an earlier chapter I referred to a newspaper interview in Indiana with Adventist evangelist G. B. Starr, in which Starr explains Bible readings: "Bible reading is another class of work. The workers go from house to house holding Bible readings with from one to twenty individuals. Last year they gave 10,000 of such Bible readings."[14] It appears that a Bible reading involved as few people or as many as would fit into a home.

3. *Social Meeting:*[15] In the mid-nineteenth century, the Methodist class meeting was changing into a weekly prayer meeting that included social dimensions. The Adventist Church also included a social meeting as part of its services. The social meeting was often held after a preaching service, sometimes midweek, but frequently on Sabbath. The social meeting allowed the congregation time to share personally the benefit they received from the sermon or Bible study presentation. At other times the social meeting was held in lieu of a sermon, as early Adventists did not have regular assigned pastors. In these situations the meeting followed the Sabbath school time.

The social meeting included prayer, testimonies, words of encouragement to one another, singing, and fellowship. The meeting was very similar to the elements contained in what we today would call a praise, prayer, and testimony service. One difference was that the social meeting was not limited to a certain number of attendees. In some cases, if the congregation was too large, the participants would divide into smaller groups to give everyone an opportunity to participate.

James White, in *Life Incidents,* provides us with a glimpse of an effective meeting: "Social meetings were marked with great solemnity. Sins were confessed with tears, and there was a general breaking down before God, and strong pleadings for pardon, and a fitness to meet the Lord at His coming. And the humble disciples of the Lord did not seek His face in vain. Before that meeting closed, hundreds testified with tears of joy that they had sought the Lord and found Him, and had tasted the sweets of sins forgiven."[16]

"During one social meeting 117 testimonies were given in 53 minutes. All right to the point."[17] A review of early Adventist articles and letters demonstrates that the social meeting was a key part of church life, and attendance was even considered a duty by some. The social meeting was the time to build community among the members through prayer and testimonies. Ellen White said it was essential for the church to have social meetings and that young ministers should be taught how to conduct social meetings.[18]

In 1882 Ellen White described such a meeting in these words: "The prayer and social meetings should be the most interesting gatherings that are held. Plans should be laid, and wisdom sought of God, to conduct these meetings so that they will be interesting and attractive. The people hunger for the bread of life. If they find it at the prayer meeting, they will go there to receive it. Long, prosy talks and prayers are out of place anywhere, and especially in the social meeting. They weary the angels as well as the people who listen to them. Our prayers should be short, and right to the point. Let the Spirit of God pervade the hearts of the worshipers, and it will sweep away all formality and dullness."[19]

The social meeting in the Adventist Church evolved, or devolved, into a prayer meeting that went from the original plan of prayer, praise, and testimony to a pastoral sermon followed by a few minutes of prayer. Today some churches don't even have a prayer meeting. If they do, only a few attend. We need to go back to the original format, which involves a more relational approach. Some of the prayer conferences of the 1990s in the Adventist Church closely reflect the characteristics of the social meeting.

4. *Open-Air Meetings/Camp Meetings:* Winning souls has always been an Adventist priority. Early Adventists preached wherever and whenever there was opportunity. Because of lack of funds to rent public buildings and because many times large public facilities were not available, meetings were conducted outside. An example was an evangelistic meeting in May of 1854 at Locke, Ingham County, Michigan. "The

schoolhouse they used would not hold half the audience, so the speaker stood in the open window and spoke both to those in the house and to a larger crowd on the grass and in their carriages."[20] In addition, large crowds would gather on the property of someone's farm or in a central public gathering place.

Tents for public meetings were a novelty, especially in the western United States in the mid-1800s. Simply by putting up a tent one could attract a crowd. Thus tents and open-air meetings were very successful. The first SDA camp meeting was held in 1868 in a maple grove on the farm of Elder E. H. Root, at Wright, Michigan. It was an outdoor meeting with the use of both open-air seating and tents. "The earlier camp meetings were planned not alone for the spiritual blessing of believers but as evangelistic efforts for the general public; therefore, it was the policy to change the place of meeting each year; and much of the preaching, especially in the evening and on Sunday, was with this purpose in mind. This plan was advocated by Mrs. White as late as 1900."[21]

5. *Sabbath Worship Service:* A vital part of Adventism was the Sabbath services. These usually involved a Sabbath school of Bible study, prayer, and fellowship, with outreach and learning leadership skills as an essential part. The service that followed was a preaching service or a social meeting.

6. *Personal Visitation:* Today we use the term *friendship evangelism* in reflecting this point. The key ingredients involve establishing social relationships with attending non-members, neighbors, and work associates, with the goal in mind of meeting their needs and introducing them to Jesus through Bible study and personal experience.

7. *Personal Prayer and Bible Study:* The Bible states that Jesus spent much time in prayer. If Christians are to grow spiritually, or have an effective ministry, they must spend time daily with God.

A local church that incorporates the stated seven items will have a balanced program of nurture and outreach. There will be opportunities for the Holy Spirit to make an impact on their ministry. Not only will the Spirit move and act in the personal lives of the members, but lives will be changed as the plans of God are followed. Ellen White stated it well when she said, "Surrender all your plans to Him, to be carried out or given up as His providence shall indicate. Thus day by day you may be giving your life into the hands of God, and thus your life will be molded more and more after the life of Christ."[22]

I talked to one of the pastors in southern Oregon recently. He was excited about the baptisms and increasing number of small groups in his church during the past few months. My friend told me that usually he has to encourage new groups to start. However, his members have now seen the benefit of the small groups. Following the recent reaping crusade one of the men in his church said, "We must place the new members and interests in small groups. We don't have enough groups, so we need to start three more." Other members followed his lead and, on their own, organized enough groups to meet the current needs of the church. My pastor friend told me it was exciting to watch his members take the lead. The equipping, mentoring, and vision-casting had paid off!

---

[1] Ellen G. White, *Life Sketches,* p. 25.

[2] *Ibid.,* p. 43.

[3] John Dillenberger and Claude Welch, *Protestant Christianity* (New York: Charles Scribner and Sons, 1954), pp. 129-136.

[4] B. Waugh and T. Mason, *The Works of the Reverend John Wesley* (1832), vol. 7, p. 12.

[5] A. J. Wollen, *Miracles Happen in Group Bible Study,* p. 36.

[6] E. G. White, *Gospel Workers,* p. 193.

[7] ———, *This Day With God* (Washington, D.C.: Review and Herald Pub. Assn., 1979), p. 11.

[8] Wollen, pp. 36, 37.

[9] E. G. White, *Evangelism,* p. 115.

[10] ———, *Testimonies,* vol. 9, pp. 82, 83.

[11] ———, *Counsels to Parents and Teachers* (Mountain View, Calif.: Pacific Press Pub. Assn., 1913), p. 551.

[12] ———, *Testimonies,* vol. 9, p. 126.

[13] ———, *Early Writings* (Washington, D.C.: Review and Herald Pub. Assn., 1882), p. 282.

[14] G. B. Starr, in Wabash, Indiana, *Plain Dealer,* Oct. 1, 1886, p. 5.

[15] Much of the research information shared concerning social meetings is taken from a research project by Russell Burrill entitled "A Biblical and Adventist Historical Study of Small Groups as a Basis for Mission," May 1996.

[16] James White, *Life Incidents* (Battle Creek, Mich.: Steam Press of SDA Pub. Assn., 1868), vol. 1, p. 167. Here James White is speaking of social meetings during the Millerite movement.

[17] J. N. Loughborough, *Miracles in My Life* (Phoenix, Ariz.: Leaves of Autumn Books, 1987), p. 88.

[18] E. G. White, "Labor at the Camp-Meetings," *Signs of the Times,* May 17, 1883.

[19] ———, "Christian Work," *Review and Herald,* Oct. 10, 1882.

[20] Arthur W. Spalding, *Origin and History of Seventh-day Adventists* (Washington, D.C.: Review and Herald Pub. Assn., 1962), vol. 2, p. 7.

[21] *Ibid.,* pp. 17, 18.

[22] E. G. White, *Steps to Christ* (Washington, D.C.: Review and Herald Pub. Assn., 1982), p. 70.

Chapter Eight

Will the Real Church Model Please Stand Up!

The late 1980s and 1990s will be remembered by some as a period of transition in denominational life. The baby boomer desire to "do church different," along with the church's desire to attract the boomers, has contributed to the pilot testing of new methods. In addition, there has been a resurgence of going back to the New Testament model to fix the problem of low lay involvement in evangelism and low church attendance in many parts of the world. These factors have moved the church from a "cookie cutter," top-down approach to ministry toward a wider variety of styles and methods.

The new emphasis on community has resulted in a renewed emphasis on small groups meeting in private homes. There are many books and seminars regarding what is the best way to structure this ministry. Some pastors and lay leaders are confused about what many of the terms and concepts mean. Here is a summary of some of the small group models being discussed and some of the relevant terminology.

Small Group Structures

The traditional approach to small groups has tended to make small groups secondary and large group meetings primary. Small groups have been relegated to prayer meeting and to the Sabbath school class before the worship service. Unfortunately, not enough time is usually allocated to these classes. Also, the emphasis has been on objective Bible study, with little time spent on building social relationships.

The traditional approach also tends to be *program-centered.* Life in the church revolves around programs to meet needs of the members and to minister to the unchurched. Relational groups are secondary. Churches with this style are sometimes called PBD churches (program-based design).

The *seeker-targeted* church believes that God has called the church to connect the lost with Jesus Christ. Everything the church does and every dollar spent must contribute to the goal of reaching non-Christians. The worship service is designed with the nonchurched in mind. The music, format, language, etc., are all adapted to the needs of the unchurched. The main goal is not so much to nourish the saints as to provide a non-threatening environment for newcomers. This is a worship-centered approach: church life revolves around the weekend and midweek worship services. Other aspects of church life, including small groups, may be important, but they are secondary.

Metachurch. This terminology comes from Carl George. Meta is a prefix from the Greek that has to do with change. It occurs in words such as metamorphosis, metabolism, and in the Greek word *metanoia,* repentance, which refers to the change that takes place with spiritual conversion. Thus a metachurch is a church in transition—a church that is becoming what God wants His church to be.

This is more a philosophy than a structure. A key issue is attempting to understand more fully how the family of God should relate to one another and to God, and how the church is to be staffed and structured organizationally. One of the main duties of the metachurch pastor is the formation or equipping of lay leaders who provide care and ministry to the church family and to the unchurched. A critical part of the metachurch is the goal of conversion growth by the Holy Spirit working through lay-led home discipleship centers. All ministry functions are decentralized to the home groups, and the clergy are then freed to focus on training and lay leadership development.

Metachurches are churches that examine their ministry and structure to determine if they need to change to fit the New Testament model of church life. Metachurch proponents state that it is not a program, a structure, or a system, but a way of thinking. How each church will look at the end of the transition process is uncertain, but small groups are usually a central component in metachurch philosophy.*

Many churches are *program-based with small groups;* they have included small home groups as part of their "program." In attempting to meet the needs of the various personality types in the congregation, they have continued their regular programs, but with the addition of small groups as one option. The church is still basically program-centered, however. In such a setting the small group program usually struggles because the pastor is seen as director or overseer of all the programs, and time limitations do not allow the pastor to concentrate on any one aspect of ministry. Groups are simply one arm of church life.

Another familiar word used to describe small group churches today is transition. A *transitional church* family has decided that they want their ministry to revolve around small groups, but currently they are still a program-based church. These churches are in the process of restructuring so that small groups provide the services that the many programs once provided. This is an extremely difficult task, because it is a new and strange model for most churches. In a small-group-based church everyone belongs to a group, and church life is in the small groups and not the programs. All else is secondary. Many churches struggle with this transition, because not all current members want this change to occur.

A pure *cell church* is one that has virtually no programs. Church life occurs in the cell. Every member of the church belongs to a small group. All ministry functions of nurture to the members and outreach occur through a small group. The pastor's role is to train and equip the members to perform ministry in the context of groups, not to do the ministry himself. Group members minister to the needs of one another whenever they are sick, in the hospital, grieving, discouraged, in need of food or clothing, or needing Bible instruction.

Large group meetings are held periodically for training and for inspiration. There are periodic rallies or other special events, but only if they do not conflict with group life. Nothing competes with the groups, not even board meetings. The church family worships together on the weekend, but there are no other regular weekly programs.

These are some of the current small-group buzzwords and concepts being used in discussions of small groups. All sides in the discussion agree that small groups, large meetings, and programs all have their place in the church, and that the laity must be equipped for ministry. But there is disagreement over the exact balance of emphasis on the various concepts.

Each congregation must determine the correct model for itself through prayer, study of the Bible and the writings of Ellen White, and an honest evaluation of their current church life. When God speaks through the Holy Spirit to the entire congregation regarding local church ministry, it will be owned and not imposed. However, it is obvious from the evidence that the church must be centered in community, which involves all members of the congregation in some aspect of small groups, as well as in large group ministry (current examples of how to do this will be in a later chapter).

Neither program-based churches nor small-group-based churches are inherently unbiblical, in my opinion. Both large and small group ministry is needed, as long as balance is maintained. What is important is that every church member should be using their gifts in ministry, that all belong to some type of small group, that large group meetings be inspirational so as to uplift those who attend, and that church life revolve around community and ministry. If the congregation is seeking the power of the Holy Spirit and doing God's will, then I believe God will honor their efforts and bless them.

Group Formats in the Seventh-day Adventist Church

Within the Seventh-day Adventist Church the entire range of small group formats is found, with the possible exception of the pure cell church model, which is common mainly in countries in which there is persecution and in areas where there are very few members. In traditional Adventist churches the Sabbath school class functions as the only small group component of church life. Most Adventist churches are program-based, with small groups as one option. In both of these formats some churches have worked extremely hard at making the Sabbath school class contribute to ministry and community in the local church. Many of these churches have eliminated most of the Sabbath school program time to give more class time. In addition, many churches have introduced into the class some new elements: a sharing time to develop social relationships, outreach projects, and more practical application of the Bible doctrines taught in the lessons.

One style that has been used by many churches is what has been named Sabbath School Action Units (to be discussed in a future chapter). In addition, some churches have combined both Sabbath school class time and weekly home-based small groups in place of the traditional prayer meeting, which is usually low in attendance.

Many Adventist churches are currently in transition from a program-based ministry to a small-group-based ministry, and are attempting to provide a small group experience for every church member.

Currently there are several pilot cell churches in the denomination. The North American Division Evangelism Institute at Andrews University and the North American Division Adult Ministries Department are both giving leadership in this area. The next few years should provide some helpful data on the use of the cell model in ministry.

I am excited that members and leaders are praying and seeking God's leading regarding His will for their local church, and coming up with an interesting diversity of ideas. When honest searching occurs, God can and will do great and exciting things for His church. This is a sign of the movement of the Holy Spirit. The bones are beginning to rattle!

---

* Carl F. George, *Prepare Your Church for the Future* (Tarrytown, N.Y.: Fleming H. Revell, 1991), p. 57ff.

Chapter Nine

Small Groups 101 —The Basics

I was conducting a small group training seminar when a young woman approached me and said, "I hope this is a basic course for beginners, because I need lots of help! Please explain what a small group is." Let's tackle that question first.

Definition of a Small Group

There are various definitions of a small group. Here are several examples:

"A cell is a small group with an ideal size of 8 to 15 people who meet together on a regular basis for worship, Bible study, outreach, discipleship, and prayer."[1]

"A small group within the church is a voluntary, intentional gathering of three to twelve people regularly meeting together with the shared goal of mutual Christian edification and fellowship."[2]

"A small group is an intentional, face-to-face gathering of 3 to 12 people, on a regular time schedule with the common purpose of discovering and growing in the abundant life of Christ."[3]

Some of these definitions ignore the important element of outreach. In fact I have attended nationwide small group training events in which small groups were seen as primarily for nurture, while outreach was ignored. This is a serious error. As we have already seen, outreach is implied in Acts 2:46, 47, which speaks of the house-to-house activity of the disciples followed by new accessions to the faith. Ellen White also states that small groups are for both outreach and nurture: "The formation of small companies as a basis of Christian effort is a plan that has been presented before me by One who cannot err. If there is a large number in the church, let the members be formed into small companies, to work not only for the church members but for unbelievers also."[4]

The following is a definition that I believe incorporates all the necessary elements: A small group is an intentional, face-to-face gathering of 3 to 12 people, meeting on a regular schedule, with the common purpose of developing relationships, meeting felt needs of group members, growing spiritually, and laying plans to lead others to accept Jesus as Lord and Saviour of their lives.

The definition of a small group must grow out of the core values or elements of a small group meeting: to develop and build community; and community is relationships. The following four relationships are key to a successful small group:

1. *God-to-Person Relationship:* The group should focus on what God wants to happen to the members individually and be sensitive to His touch in their lives.

2. *Person-to-God Relationship:* Individual response to the moving of God's Spirit is a primary part of group life. Group members must be aware of the Holy Spirit touching the lives of group members so they can be supportive. As the Spirit impresses members to respond, ordinary people will do extraordinary things for God.

3. *Person-to-Person Relationship:* The response of members to God will affect the way they relate to one another. As they grow in the Spirit they will be supportive of one another, pray for each other, assist with personal needs, be more understanding and forgiving, and desire for others to have the same experience.

4. *Person-to-World Relationship:* A group cannot be spiritually whole and not reach out to others beyond the circle. God has called people to "gather together," but He has also told them to "go." God calls for groups to help fulfill this commission. Group leaders must model outreach. This is one critical factor in the success of a group.

Group life arises from these core elements. As seen in a previous chapter, Acts 2:41-47 provides the agenda of activities for all of church life. Let's apply the principles to a small group meeting. The items listed are:

ACTS 2	GROUP FORMAT
• Apostles' doctrine	Bible study
• Fellowship	Personal sharing, social interaction

• Prayer	Prayer time
• Breaking bread together	Worshiping, eating together
• Had everything in common	Meet personal needs of group members
• People were baptized	Outreach and mission

Based on this information, all small groups will have five common components: loving, learning, deciding, doing, and praying. *Loving* involves listening and sharing one's personal story. *Learning* comes by studying information and the Bible together. *Deciding* involves making group decisions about what to do with the children, what the group will do with their time together, when to multiply the group, and other such matters. Much of the deciding is done in the initial meetings, and is not a major ongoing focus of the group. *Doing* is the mission of the group. What is its purpose? What is the group trying to accomplish? What is its outreach ministry? *Praying* is something that should permeate group life.

As far as the actual group meeting agenda is concerned, there are four main components. These agenda items are sharing, Bible study, prayer, and mission. Every type of group follows this same agenda. *Sharing* includes loving and deciding. *Bible study* includes learning. *Mission* is outreach to others, which is the doing. *Prayer* is seeking the power of God in all aspects of group life. Of course, there is some overlap of components. Different kinds of groups will spend different amounts of time on each item. For example, a group whose concentration is on sharing would spend less time in Bible study, mission, and prayer. An outreach Bible study group might spend less time on sharing and prayer.

Below is a sample agenda for two different types of 1.5-hour group meetings:

Fellowship Group	**Outreach Bible Study Group**
Sharing—50 minutes	Sharing—20 minutes
Bible Study—25 minutes	Bible Study—55 minutes
Prayer/Mission—15 minutes	Mission/Prayer—15 minutes

Every group must, of course, be flexible enough to meet the emergent needs of the group and to follow the leading of the Holy Spirit. There is no one right way to organize and lead a group. This structure is only a beginning point. Still, the group will follow a basic outline, though the sequence and terminology may vary somewhat from group to group, which will include these four vital ingredients: sharing questions, Bible study, mission, and prayer. Let's look at each of these in turn.

Sharing Questions

In order for the group to be successful, it is important that each member be involved in the discussion and willing to share openly. In order to set the stage for each meeting, the group needs to begin with a time of sharing. This sharing time gets everyone relaxed and talking about their week and personal life in a nonthreatening environment. It helps the group to be aware of each other's needs, and it gets the quiet group members involved right away in the group process, so that they will continue to talk during the study time.

The group leader begins with prayer, then says, "Let's talk about our week. What happened in your life since our last meeting?" After the members have had time to talk about their week, the group leader asks a question that gets the group members better acquainted with one another, with the purpose of establishing closer relationships. For example, "Jesus told His disciples one day that they needed to take a break from their work and rest. What do you like to do for rest and relaxation?"

A key point to remember regarding sharing questions is that they must be nonthreatening, allowing the members to share their personal story. No special knowledge of the Bible or any other topic should be required. Sharing time should be nonjudgmental, simple, laid-back, and fun!

Sharing time has several benefits. It gets everyone involved and gives them an opportunity to get acquainted, deepen relationships, and make new friends. It provides an opportunity for the group members to become aware of and appreciate the uniqueness of one another.

There are generally five types of sharing questions that a group may participate in during the lifetime of the group. These types are:

Past-Tense Sharing Questions: These are questions that group members share about their personal history. The questions assist in understanding the life experience and background of fellow members. Past-tense questions are especially helpful in the beginning stages of a group. Examples would be: Did you attend church as a child? Which denomination? What was your favorite game as a child? What is the funniest thing that ever happened at the table in your childhood? How was your home heated when you were growing up?

Present-Tense Sharing Questions: These are questions that assist the members in talking about what is currently happening in their lives.

Examples are: What is your favorite current hobby? What is one thing that someone did for you this week that you appreciated? Where is your favorite place?

Future-Tense Sharing Questions: These questions give the members an opportunity to talk about their hopes and dreams for the future. Examples are: Where would you like to go on your next vacation? How would you like to be remembered at the end of your life?

Affirmation Sharing Questions: These questions give the members opportunity to share positive things about one another. Examples are: How has the group been the most helpful to you? What quality do you like best in each person in the group?

Accountability Sharing Questions: This type of question is used only if the members have agreed to hold each other mutually accountable for Christian living. Examples are: How has your prayer and Bible study been this past week? As a parent, have you taken quality time each day with your children this past week?

There are certain important guidelines that leaders must follow in regard to the sharing questions:

1. After asking the question, ask for a volunteer to begin. Never go around the circle and put someone on the spot. The leader may need to begin first to model the question.
2. Allow people the choice not to speak if they choose. Say something like "Who would like to be next?"; "It's OK to not share if that's your choice"; "If you feel you want to pass tonight, that's OK."
3. Choose questions that are not threatening.
4. Do not ask for opinions on controversial topics, such as abortion, capital punishment, etc.
5. Do not ask questions that cause people to be negative about themselves or life. The goal is a positive experience, giving the members opportunity to know one another better and minister to one another.

Bible Study

In Christian groups the learning/discussing time should be based on the Scriptures. Depending on the type of group, other materials may be used, but the Bible needs to be the foundation. A grief recovery group, for example, may use a contemporary book as its main focus, but the Bible should be a key resource.

In the small group the study time is inductive Bible study, which is discussion-based. The leader facilitates the discussion, but does not do all the talking. The leader guides the group in discovering the truths to be learned. This style is the opposite of the seminar approach, in which there is a teacher who shares and answers questions and allows discussion when called for or as there is time. However, a group leader does at times teach, and must always give leadership to the discussion, so that it will not become a gabfest of personal ideas or a pooling of ignorance. The teacher must study and prepare in order to guide the discussion gently without dominating the process.

An inductive Bible study has three parts to each study. First there is *observation:* What does it say? What is the context and background of the passage? The group members simply list the facts and gain as much understanding of the passage as possible. Second, there is *interpretation:* What does it mean? This involves reviewing the historical and textual context and asking what the text meant when it was originally written. Third is *application*: What parallels do we find today with the original context? How does it apply to us today? One asks, So what? What difference does it make to me today?

The ultimate goal of small group Bible study is application. One must always remember that Scripture is not just for learning, but for living. If someone in your group is in the middle of divorce proceedings, they will be more concerned about how Jesus, through the power of the Holy Spirit, can assist them right now than in understanding Jesus' genealogy.

A key question usually is what materials should be used. Experience has shown that it is best for a beginning group to use printed material and study guides, as opposed to leader-prepared material. These guides are usually written by someone who has experience in small group life, and the study guides are designed to help the group follow a pattern to ensure a more positive experience.

Mission

Every group must have a well-defined purpose and outreach strategy that is understood and owned by the group members. It is critical that group members understand the reason for their existence as a group and feel a sense of ownership of group life. Experience has shown that without an outreach strategy, the focus of the group will turn inward, the excitement and fulfillment of the group members will decline, and group life will stagnate and deteriorate.

I saw this happen in a church I visited recently. I met with the small group leaders for a training and question/answer session. Alice asked me why I thought her small group stagnated and died. Her group began with six members excited about studying, praying, and fellowshipping together. Together they established goals, but after eight months interest had waned and the group had ceased to exist. After a brief discussion I discovered that after two months of meeting, Alice's group changed its focus. They decided to let no one new into the group; they dropped all outreach because everyone was too busy; and they began centering on their own needs rather than the needs of others. Alice told me that the group members were afraid new people would destroy their close-knit community. The group violated the divine principle that reaching out to others gives life to all who are part of the process.

A thriving group will reach out to non-Christians, to Christians who do not have a growing relationship with Jesus Christ, or to those of other denominations who are searching for a deeper understanding of Scripture.

Certain types of groups are outreach groups automatically by their design and purpose. Other groups, such as a Christian prayer group, or a group of Adventists studying the book *The Great Controversy*, may need to formulate an outreach strategy or project in order to keep their group healthy and to fulfill the scriptural mandate.

Prayer

Prayer is the lifeblood of the group. Prayer bonds group members together, strengthens members for daily life, and undergirds the working of the Holy Spirit in the group. Prayer strengthens group relationships, assists members in developing a devotional life, enables members to minister to one another, and builds faith as members see God meeting the daily needs of those in the group.

It is safe to assume that some in the group have never before prayed privately, and some have never prayed publicly. Others are scared to pray out loud and might never join a group if they think they might be put on the spot. A good rule to follow is to let the group members know that they will never be asked to pray out loud. Prayer time must always be voluntary. There are, however, several ideas that a group leader can use to involve the entire group in prayer.

1. Provide written prayers for all the members to read out loud together at the end of the prayer time. Use the Lord's Prayer; the twenty-third psalm; or a written prayer.

2. Give every member a written-out passage of Scripture and invite anyone who wants to read it out loud during the prayer time to do so.

3. Distribute paper and pencils and ask the members to write out a sentence prayer and read it during the prayer time.

4. Make a statement and ask the members to fill in the blank with one or two words. An example would be "Lord, help me . . ." or "Lord, thank You for . . ."

5. Suggest that the group members pray by category. Offer sentence prayers of praise to God, sentence prayers asking God to meet the needs of those outside your group, or sentence prayers asking God to meet the needs of those within your group.

6. Have a period of silent prayer.

Usually at the beginning of the group meeting, the leader or a group member will say a prayer. During the main meeting, either at the end or during the sharing time, the members will have their time of prayer together. Usually this is conversational prayer. The prayers are short—one or two sentences. A person can pray more than once. The group does not go around the circle, but the prayers are spontaneous and voluntary.

The group should keep a prayer journal of requests and God's answers. It can also be helpful to form prayer partners once the group members have bonded with one another and are comfortable with the idea.

Types of Small Groups

There are many types of small groups. Each group follows the format discussed above of sharing, Bible study, prayer, and mission. The difference is in the emphasis and time spent on each item. Some of the most common types of groups are:

1. A *fellowship group* is designed for social interaction. The group time may not follow the four-step outline given above very closely. They may get excited about relationships and group activities, such as potlucks, shopping, picnics, hikes, trips to the zoo, etc. This group is especially helpful for new members, the lonely, singles, and those who love people and having a good time. A fellowship group must intentionally develop an outreach project for the group to do together, or outreach will be overlooked. The weakness of fellowship groups is that they may get so caught up in social activities that Bible study and prayer are overlooked.

2. A *Bible study group* is for those who like to study the Bible and other books along with other Christians in order to grow in their knowledge of a particular topic. This group may study a book of the Bible, or a topic such as last-day events, angels, etc. The weakness here is that the group can develop a sort of "we alone have the truth" attitude. This type

of group, too, needs an outreach project in order to maintain balance.

3. *Outreach groups* are designed to reach out to non-Christians, nonmembers, or nonattending church members. There are a variety of approaches. *One* example is Bible study groups. The study may be on various books of the Bible or topics such as angels, life of Jesus, etc. The Homes of Hope program on the books of John and Revelation that was developed in the Oregon Conference of Seventh-day Adventists in the late 1980s and early 1990s is an example.

A *second* type of outreach group is one that is sometimes called pathway or redemptive friendship groups. They are called pathway because they meet personal needs and direct people down the path toward Jesus. These groups do not focus on books of the Bible but on needs. An example is MOMS, mothers of preschool children. Another may be a men's or women's breakfast group in which the focus is on friendships and the fact that Jesus can make a difference in the issues of daily life.

A *third* type of outreach group is one designed to meet the needs of those who were once Christians or who currently are sporadic attendees. The purpose is to reacquaint them with Jesus. A *fourth* type is seeker groups. These are groups designed with secular people in mind. The group may be for atheists or those simply ignorant of religious themes and concepts.

The weakness of outreach groups is that they may focus on numerical growth rather than the spiritual growth of the members.

4. *Task/ministry groups* are outreach and nurture groups that do not spend the majority of their time sitting in a circle. In fact many task groups meet only once a month to spend two hours in the circle, and the other weeks they meet for a short time of sharing, Bible study, and prayer, then turn to the chosen task. One example is a literature task group that gives literature door-to-door, manages literature newsboxes and public display racks, etc. Other examples may be the Pathfinder leaders, choir members, or Sabbath school division leaders and assistants. These individuals meet weekly or bimonthly to discuss their ministry, share and support one another, have a brief study together, pray, and do ministry together.

Task groups need to look for outreach opportunities. For the Pathfinders it may be involving non-Adventist youth and their parents. For the children's Sabbath school it may be visiting non-Adventist parents whose children attend Sabbath school or other get-acquainted activities.

The theme of a task/ministry group is that God has given everyone a spiritual gift and it needs to be used in ministry. The weakness of this type of group is that the task becomes more important than relationships, Bible study, or prayer.

5. *Support groups* are designed for individuals with special needs. These needs are usually short-term, and then the person joins another type of group. Examples are divorce, grief recovery, and addictions (alcohol, drugs, tobacco, eating disorders, etc.) and similar types of needs. *The groups are for support and not for therapy. If the individual needs therapy, it should be received from a professional Christian counselor.* The group members are aware of their mutual struggles, but this is not the focus of the group. The group focuses upon friendship, studying the Bible as a source of assistance, and praying for each other. Often a relevant book or other material is used as a supplement to the Bible.

I have visited support groups that had individuals attending with a variety of needs, including bulimia, alcohol addiction, divorce recovery, and tobacco addiction. The group members shared how their week had gone, then shared a Bible study centering on how God was the solution to their needs. The group members ended their meeting by joining hands and standing in a circle, praying for one another.

The weakness of support groups is that the members may tend to focus upon their individual needs rather than upon the power of the Holy Spirit and being re-created in Jesus.

6. *Prayer groups* spend the majority of their time in prayer, although there is also Bible study and sharing. The members usually have prayer partners, prayer chains, or networks, and are willing to pray as needed for those situations and circumstances that are brought to their attention.

The weakness of prayer groups is there is a danger to view others as unspiritual if they do not belong to a prayer group or if they do not pray as much as group members do.

7. A *covenant group* is one that agrees among the members that they want to have a balance in the use of their group time focusing upon the four ingredients of sharing, Bible study, outreach ministry, and prayer. Usually the group studies a book of the Bible or a biblical topic. The group members have an open group policy and invite new people to join the group on a weekly basis. During their prayer time the members pray for new people to come each week.

This type of group is a popular one because it incorporates all aspects of a small group in a manner that meets the needs of most people the easiest. In addition, it meets the biblical criteria of small group life.

The weakness of this group is that they may lose their balance and focus on one aspect of the group meeting format. In addition, they may forget to invite new people and focus on process rather than outreach. Also, a constant influx of people may prevent the group from jelling.

8. A *house church* is a small group that meets in a home rather than a church building. In the home setting all aspects of church life are usually present. On Sabbath morning there is a Sabbath school and worship service. During the week there is a small group meeting. Any board or planning meetings are held in the home setting.

In some countries that prohibit public Christian meetings, this is how church life is lived out. It is also an outreach strategy in some countries. When I was in Brazil conducting small group training several years ago, I discovered some of the members developing plans to plant new churches using this strategy. In North America our branch Sabbath schools were based on the same premise. It is time, I believe, that we begin using small groups as a church planting strategy.

The weakness of the house church is that it can become isolated from the larger community of the church, forgetting the need to function within denominational guidelines and cooperate with the conference. Independent churches have on occasion taken a radical direction that led into unsound doctrine.

9. A *cell church* is a church where all the members belong to a small group. All of church life occurs in the cell. There are usually very few programs, and nothing is allowed to compete with the cell, including board meetings. Even the weekly worship service is secondary to cell life. A purist in the cell church concept believes that the only biblical model is the cell church model and that the traditional program-based model is not biblically correct. There are many churches outside North America that follow this model, but it is hard to find one in North America that has perfected this philosophy; however, many individuals and organizations are working hard on this concept that some say is the church of the future.

The weakness of the cell church is that there may develop a belief among the members that other small group models are invalid. An elitist attitude can develop if one is not careful.

10. *Sabbath school action units* are based upon the premise that the Adventist Church already has a built-in small group philosophy and structure that is not being used to its full capacity. The premise is that the purpose of the Sabbath school is fellowship, ministry training, Bible study, outreach (local and worldwide), and prayer support; and since these are the biblical ingredients for a small group format, they should be incorpo-

rated into the Sabbath school every Sabbath morning in each class. The classes are given a minimum of one hour in which to follow the small group format of sharing, study, prayer, and working on an outreach project. Sometimes the class project may be a small home group during the week. The home group and Sabbath school class can then work together as a unit for more success. Several conferences in North America, such as Michigan and Upper Columbia, have concentrated upon this type of small group. We will discuss this concept in more detail in a future chapter.

The weakness of the Sabbath school action unit is that in some cases the location of the class and the time available are not conducive to healthy group life. Often the members sit in pews together with other classes in the sanctuary. Because of inadequate time and location, the group interaction is not as bonding as it could be. This leads to discouragement and lack of participation by the members, and a negative attitude toward small groups in general.

Several have taken the preceding 10 group types and divided them under main categories for easier identification. For example, the terms of Mary groups and Martha groups are used based upon the Bible story of Mary sitting at the feet of Jesus while Martha fixed the meal. Those who sit in the weekly circle groups for daily nurture purposes belong to Mary groups. Those who prefer action rather than weekly circle groups belong to Martha groups.

MARY GROUPS	MARTHA GROUPS
Fellowship groups	Some outreach groups
Bible study groups	House church
Outreach groups	Sabbath school action units
Prayer groups	
Support groups	
Covenant groups	

Here is another three-way division of groups:

TASK GROUPS	FELLOWSHIP GROUPS	BIBLE STUDY
Outreach	Fellowship	Bible study
Support	Covenant	Sabbath school action unit
Sabbath school action unit	Prayer	
House church		

Others have called the groups community groups (those that bridge to the community); disciplemaking groups (those that assist Christians); and serving groups (those that provide ministry opportunities to utilize spiritual gifts).

There may be some overlap in these categories, One must also keep in mind that the various types of groups follow the same agenda or format of sharing, Bible study, prayer, and mission; however, the amount of time may vary depending upon the type of group and its mission. The following diagrams illustrate this principle.

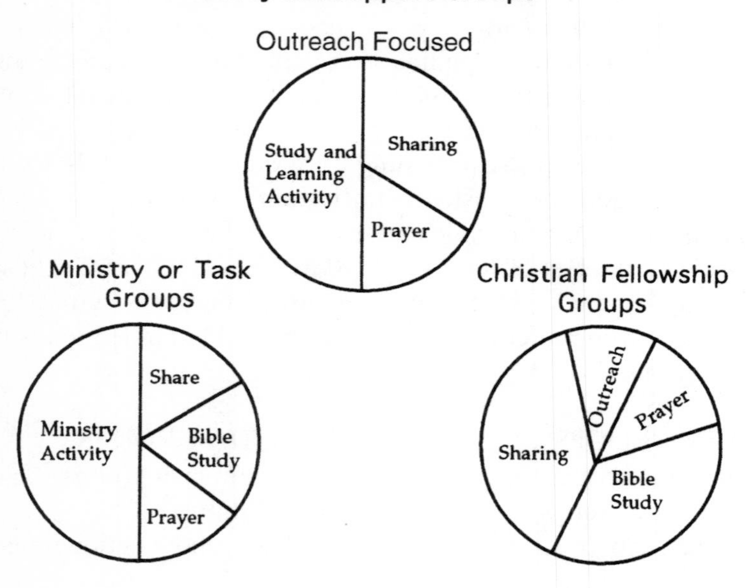

A Healthy Small Group

A healthy small group will be one that is open to everyone no matter what their need may be. It is true that at times the special needs of someone may dictate that another type of group may better meet their need, but the group leader will assist that person in joining the group that is best for them. One must also keep in mind the importance of the affinity factor—that is that people with similar needs draw strength and support from seeking God together. A healthy group would look something like this:

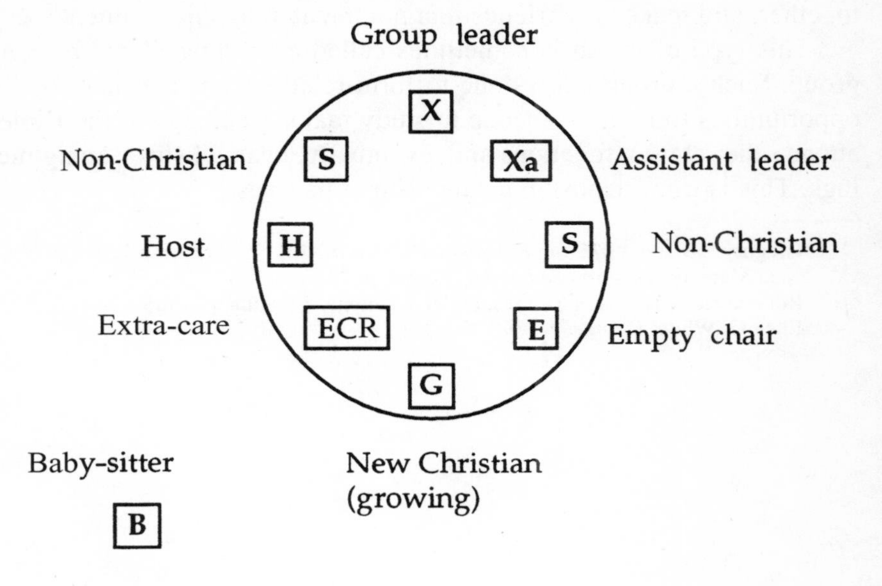

X = group leader
Xa = assistant group leader
H = host
B = baby-sitter/children's ministry leader
S = non-Christian
G = new Christian (growing)
ECR = extra-care-required person
E = empty chair (always room for one more; and a safe place to visit)

The next chapter will provide job descriptions and a further explanation of these leadership and participant descriptions.

Kathy's two sons had left home. One was married; the other was in college. As she adjusted to her new lifestyle, Kathy thought that a small group studying various biblical topics with other "empty-nesters" would be an excellent outreach. She looked around her and discovered that neighbors, work associates, friends from church, and other general acquaintances were in the same stage of life. She invited them to join a small group with others like themselves. The affinity factor was not their religious beliefs or backgrounds but their stage in life. This provided for a group of women to support one another, pray together, study the Bible together, and make new friends in a nonthreatening environment.

This type of group is sometimes called a "pathway" or "bridging" group. Such a group allows one to form relationships that later provide opportunities to invite someone to study major teachings of the Bible or attend other church functions and, eventually, evangelistic reaping meetings. This is true friendship evangelism at its finest!

---

[1] Gregory Lawson, *Christian Educational Journal* XIII, No. 3 (Spring 1993), p. 67.
[2] Neal McBride, *How to Lead Small Groups,* p. 24.
[3] Roberta Hestenes, class lectures, Fuller Theological Seminary, 1986.
[4] Ellen G. White, *Evangelism,* p. 115.

Chapter Ten

Small Groups 201 —Understanding Your Group

Many Adventist lay leaders have taught prophecy seminars or Sabbath school classes or have preached a sermon. One question they frequently ask is What is the difference between this and a small group meeting? The following points help to answer this question.

1. The small group meeting is normally held in a home rather than the church or public building. I have attended meetings in a funeral home, in offices at lunch hour, and in a restaurant. Any nonthreatening location will work.

2. The seating arrangement is with chairs in a circle rather than in a row. A living room or kitchen table is an excellent location. It is key that no one sit outside the circle, or the dynamic will be lost.

3. Group meetings are usually one night per week for 90 to 120 minutes in length. It is important to begin and end on time, or some members may stop attending. Members need their sleep, and some may need to get children to bed.

4. Rather than a prepared lecture by a teacher, there is a leader-guided discussion. Nevertheless, preparation is still essential. Some group leaders make the mistake of not studying the material before the meeting. A leader who does not understand the material cannot guide the discussion. At times it is necessary for the leader to assume the role of teacher for a short period of time. To say that teaching is never an aspect of a small group is not reality. But the leader is a facilitator, not a lecturer.

5. The focus of the study time is developing interpersonal rela-

tionships and the application of biblical knowledge to everyday life. Understanding Scripture and knowing doctrine is important, but life application is very important in a small group setting. Remember, Scripture is not only for learning but also for living.

6. It is important to call for decision responses throughout the group time together, but not to the point of pressure that causes some to stop attending. The key is to keep the members coming to give the Holy Spirit opportunity to convict hearts.

7. The maximum number of participants in many small groups is approximately 12. Sometimes more than 12 can participate, depending on the type of house meeting. In contrast, a class-lecture-style approach can accommodate a larger number.

8. In a small group it is very important to be sensitive to the spiritual growth of your members and not share too much information too fast. The apostle Paul in 1 Corinthians 3:1, 2 stated, "Brothers, I could not address you as spiritual but as worldly—mere infants in Christ. I gave you milk, not solid food, for you were not ready for it" (NIV). Ellen White, commenting upon the same topic, writes, "You need not feel that all the truth is to be spoken to unbelievers on any and every occasion. You should plan carefully what to say and what to leave unsaid. This is not practicing deception; it is to work as Paul worked."*

Location and Leadership

Choosing the location of your group is critical to its success. An uncomfortably cold or warm room, noisy children, or pets can distract group members. In selecting a location, choose wisely. Careful planning should provide:

a. A comfortable atmosphere in the living room or around the kitchen table.
b. Good lighting is necessary for study and developing a warm atmosphere.
c. Arrange seating in a circle so everyone can see one another as they talk.
d. Choose a location that will provide the fewest distractions and interruptions. Children, pets, telephones, television, radios, etc., can disrupt your study group.
e. In order for some group members to attend, baby-sitting may be necessary. If a home has additional space, a volunteer may be obtained to take care of the children.

Group leader. A separate chapter will deal with leadership in small groups, so a brief job description will suffice for this section. A small group leader is the person appointed and recognized to serve the group by facilitating and enabling the group to achieve its purposes and goals. This is done in the following way.

- Attend a leadership training workshop and participate in a small group as an assistant leader or participant.
- Facilitate the weekly group meeting.
- Oversee all details of group life in and outside of the weekly meeting.
- Model and encourage participation, sharing, acceptance, and understanding among the members.
- Guide the group in developing a covenant, goals, and in carrying them out.
- Check on those who are absent from the meeting in order to encourage, meet needs, and to be aware of difficulties.
- Talk and pray weekly about the group with the assistant leader and with the host.
- Seek assistance as needed to ensure positive group life.
- Attend regular scheduled leader's meetings.

The *assistant leader* should:

- Be a prayer support and encourager for the leader.
- Facilitate the group meeting when the leader is absent.
- Assist in recruitment of new members and follow-up of absent members.
- Assist with details such as baby-sitting arrangements, completing and turning in of required report forms, and other details as needed.
- Attend monthly leader's meeting.
- Be an apprentice in training to lead a group of your own in the future.

The *host* should:

- Provide a comfortable home or location for the meeting.
- Arrange seating in the meeting room; temperature adjustments; oversee refreshments if the group has them; make sure extra Bibles, paper, study guides, pencils are available; etc.
- Answer the door and welcome the members as they arrive.
- Make sure the members' needs are met, such as location of the bathroom, drinking glasses, telephone, etc.
- Take care of distractions that may occur during the group meeting such as the doorbell, telephone, children, pets, etc.

These three positions are important to the success of a small group. However, spiritual preparation is the first and most important step. Through the power of the Holy Spirit, the least experienced individual can be dramatically effective. The spiritual success of the group is dependent, not upon the talents or abilities of the leaders, but upon their willingness to yield themselves to the will and power of God.

The Covenant

It is essential that the group come to an understanding concerning their expectations for the meeting and their relationships with one another. An agreement will solve many difficulties and prevent many problems before they start. A covenant or agreement defines group members' expectations; provides accountability to one another; enhances commitment to the group; provides a basis by which to evaluate your group's success; and establishes the purpose of the group.

At the first group meeting, the leader should share basic information with the group members and get acquainted, and tell the group that the next week they will discuss in detail the issues and agenda of their small group time together. The areas to cover at this second meeting are as follows:

- The group is a safe place to be. Members are accepted just as they are.
- No one will ever be put on the spot or intentionally embarrassed. If someone wants to talk, pray, or read, it will be their voluntary choice. The group will not go around the circle and ask anyone to do anything.
- The group members will not try to "fix" anyone, but will let the Holy Spirit change and convict people.
- The group goal is to share the experience with others. Eventually the group will multiply and form a new group under the direction of the assistant leader.
- Basic ground rules include the day to meet, the time to begin and end, the need for child care, the length of time (weeks, months) the group will meet, the importance of calling the leader if a member will miss the meeting so the group won't wait for them, and other concerns of the leader and members.
- The group should decide on the length of time to spend on the four parts of group life: sharing, study, mission, and prayer.

- The group should discuss the process of inviting new people to the group once the group has been meeting for an extended period of time.

Once the agreement is discussed, the group members should respect one another and the leader by assisting in accomplishing the details of the agreement. The following is a sample form to use in developing a group agreement.

GROUP AGREEMENT

Type of group: ________________ Purpose: ____________________

Meeting location ______________________________________

Weekday: ______________ Beginning time: _____ Closing time: _____

Our group will meet for _______________ months

Our weekly meeting schedule will be: __________________________

Individual preparation needed (group meeting only or outside of group):

____

Group leader (name and phone): ____________________________

Assistant leader (name and phone): __________________________

Host (name and phone): ____________________________________

We wish our group to be

☐ open continually to new members

☐ open for ______ weeks

Additional elements we want to be part of our group: _____________

____

Ground rules we agree to abide by:

1. We will do our best to be on time for the meetings. If we cannot attend, we will phone the leader or another member to let them know.

2. We will look for ways to assist the leaders and other members in making the group experience as positive as possible.

3. We will share our own personal feelings, but also come willing to listen to others as they share.

4. We will respect the differences in one another and not try to change them. Change is God's responsibility. Our responsibility is love, caring, acceptance, and respect.

5. What group members share in the group will be confidential.

6. Other:

Every small group has a distinct personality and set of characteristics that make it unique. Here are some tips about the covenant that are applicable to most groups, and that will make life easier for the group.

First, discuss the type of group (fellowship, support, prayer, outreach, etc.) that you are forming. The type of group is determined by its primary focus: the reason for which the group exists.

Second, let the purpose of the group arise out of the type of group. For example, the purpose of a grief recovery group may be to assist members in dealing with the issues of loss. An outreach Bible study may assist members in understanding how God can make a difference in the issues of daily life.

Third, the group should decide when they will meet and the length of the meeting. This will guarantee more participation. Some churches attempt to have all groups meet on the same night and at the same time. This option should be carefully examined to see if it will have a positive or negative effect on the attendance. It is essential to begin and end on time. In Oregon, where I live, many of the loggers leave for work at 4:00 a.m. This means that a late evening meeting usually excludes them.

Fourth, in discussing the schedule and format, determine the amount of time that will be spent on sharing, study, prayer, and discussing the mission. This will assure a balance that all the members can live with and assists the leader in keeping the group on schedule. Most groups meet for less than 2 hours per meeting, so the time is limited. In addition, the group needs to talk about how long it will meet before a transition is made and it reorganizes. I am of the opinion that, if possible, everyone in the church should be in some type of group; but periodically, say, whenever the current study material is completed, the group should provide a transition time for the members. However, if a group is multiplying and dividing by constantly adding new members, transitioning becomes an ongoing process. I would also suggest that multiplying and dividing is the healthiest way for groups to transition.

Fifth, the group should discuss whether or not there will be homework assignments. If time must be spent outside of the group in individual preparation, it may keep some from attending. Openly discuss this issue so members will not be discouraged.

Once the covenant is discussed and agreed upon, the group members will have ownership of the group, and the leader will have the permission and the responsibility to carry out the details. In addition, the covenant gives the group a tool to use in the future when they discuss how the group is doing in meeting the needs and expectations of the members.

The Leader's Meeting

Another absolute essential to a successful small group ministry is a regular leader's meeting. Experience indicates that when a group ministry is first beginning, a weekly leader's meeting is essential. Once the group ministry is established, a meeting once or twice a month is usually sufficient.

The purpose of the meeting is: (1) casting and building the vision; (2) learning skills ; (3) sharing of ideas and problems, praying together, and reporting. There are various names given to the leadership meetings and to the various segments. A common name is VHS meeting, which is an acronym for vision, huddle, and skill training. The pastor and an assigned coordinator (church member) should be present. The pastor should do the monthly vision building so the group leaders and pastor continue to "work off the same page." The reporting can be done by the lay leader and the training can be by the pastor, lay leader, guest, videotape, audiotape, book assignments, and discussion.

The leader's meeting gives the leaders support; an opportunity to share joys and frustrations; a chance to share solutions to group problems; and a time to pray together. If a leader's meeting is not held on a regular basis, it is almost guaranteed that the leaders will become discouraged and the group ministry will not flourish in the local church. Do not overlook this key ingredient. If necessary, eliminate other meetings and programs in the local church to provide time for this key element of a successful group program.

See appendix for a sample report form to use on a monthly basis to be turned in during the leader's meeting.

The Leadership Structure

Even though your group ministry may begin very small—perhaps with only one or two groups—it is essential to organize a leadership structure from the beginning that will allow you to build and expand as the number of groups in your church grows. No need to be continually reorganizing.

A simple but viable staff structure is as follows:

- Pastor as supporter and vision builder.
- Lay leader as coordinator of the overall program.
- Assistant lay coordinator.
- Coach and assistant—leaders who oversee a maximum of 10 groups.
- Small group leaders and assistants for individual groups.

Note: Each of the positions listed above will always have assistant leaders who are in training.

The structure chart would look similar to this:

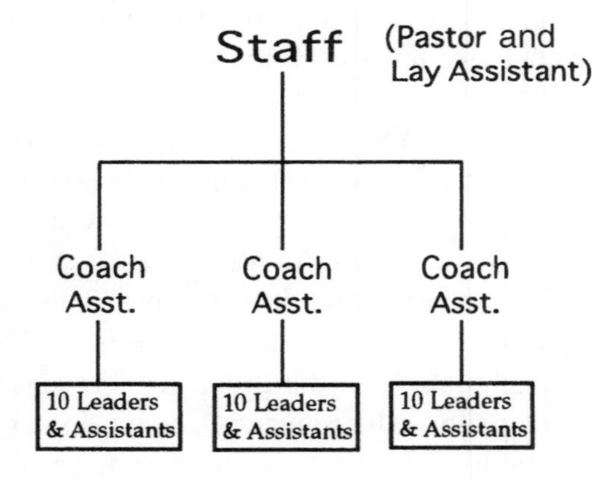

The pastor and lay member coordinator oversee the entire small group program. The church territory is divided into sections geographically. A coach (lay member) and assistant oversee a maximum of 10 group leaders within their assigned geographic section. The small group leader and assistant lead a group with usually a maximum of 12 members.

On every level of the organizational structure there will be leaders meetings and regular contact to ensure that support and problem solving are efficient and adequate.

How a Pastor Can Begin a Small Group Ministry

1. Research. Become familiar with small groups through the Scriptures, the writings of Ellen White, and books on the subject. Talk to individuals with small group experience.

2. Attend a small group training seminar and visit a church with an existing small group ministry.

3. Pray and ask God to guide you to several individuals in your church with whom to share your vision for small groups. Once you have selected these persons, invite them to attend a meeting with you in which your vision can be shared. The number invited should be no more than 10 individuals. An even number is best.

4. At your first meeting with the individuals, share your vision and ask them to meet one night a week for five weeks in which you will model a small group with them and spend some time teaching them small group principles.

5. At the end of the five weeks ask them to pray and determine if God may be asking them to be part of a small group ministry. If they say yes, then divide the group into pairs. If you had six individuals out of the 10 agree to be part of a small group ministry, then once they are paired you will have three groups of two. These two become the leader and assistant leader of a group. Ask the two to invite two or three other members of the church to be part of their group. Have them conduct a group for another five weeks.

6. At the end of the five weeks, meet with your group leaders and their assistants and plan with them how to begin a full-fledged group ministry to the community, using them as the beginning leaders. From these groups you will train leaders and multiply your groups.

7. Once the group ministry is begun, the pastor should preach about groups and their function from the Scriptures.

8. Incorporate small group experiences and prayer requests as part of the worship service. This will inspire and encourage others.

9. Include in the church newsletter and bulletin the dates, time, and locations of the groups and the names of the leaders so potential members can contact them if they want to join a group.

10. Have special consecration services for the new leaders on Sabbath mornings so the church can pray for the leaders.

11. Schedule small group training seminars on a regular basis to train the church members.

12. Continue to have leader's meetings to give the leaders the needed training and support.

13. Plan reaping crusades, baptismal classes, regular individual Bible studies, and other evangelistic activities for aiding others in making decisions for Jesus and the church.

14. Make small group ministry the central part of church life and reduce the number of board meetings and other programs to provide time for the members to be involved. This is critical for the success of the ministry. People have a limited amount of time, and the church can't do everything. So choose and plan wisely for the benefit of the church members.

How a Lay Leader Can Begin a Small Group

1. Prayerfully study information on starting and leading groups. Pray earnestly for the leading of the Holy Spirit in seeking God's wisdom and guidance.
2. Make an appointment with your pastor. Express your desire to begin a small group ministry in your home. Ask your pastor for counsel, help, and prayer support.
3. Attend a small group training seminar or listen to tapes or read books on the topic.
4. Select a fellow church member to be your assistant leader. Meet together on a regular basis, asking God for guidance as you plan your small group.
5. If you need a place to meet other than your home, ask another member if you can use their home.
6. Make a prospect list and invite others to be a part of your group.
7. The leader and assistant leader should request a monthly meeting to inform the pastor of what is happening in the group, ask questions, and pray together.
8. As opportunities arise, share group experiences with the church members on Sabbath.
9. Recruit and train potential small group leaders, incorporating them into the monthly meeting with the pastor.
10. Continue to pray and seek the power of the Holy Spirit as the small group ministry grows.

A church of 130 members in Michigan decided on an outreach strategy involving small groups in Sabbath school, door-to-door visitation, individual Bible studies, and friendliness and caring. The plan was to invite people to take Bible studies. Those invited included friends, acquaintances, names from general visitation, and people who had responded to mailed Bible request cards. Next the Sabbath school members organized their traditional classes into small groups that met during the regular class time and a portion of the Sabbath school program time. Some of the members invited their friends to a small group Bible study in their home; others gave individual Bible studies. The goal was to eventually get the Bible study interests to attend the small group Sabbath school class.

What happened? In five years there were 60 baptisms! The church grew from 130 members to 200 members. In one of those years a small group Sabbath school class prayed for 15 baptisms, and God provided 16! The members say that prayer is a key ingredient! The members prayed a minimum of three times a day for their Bible study friends, and God blessed with a rich harvest.

---

* Ellen G. White, *Evangelism,* p. 125.

Chapter Eleven

Small Groups 301 —Off and Running

Jennifer told me that the first night of her small group meeting she was scared to death! She wasn't sure what to say or not say. She did not want to hurt anyone's feelings. She wanted the group to be successful. She did not want to embarrass herself or anyone else. After much prayer and antacid for her stomach she was ready to begin. The meeting went well, and Jennifer was off and running.

What should you say on your opening night? How do you invite someone to visit and try the group out?

Inviting a Visitor

The key to a successful small group is a personal invitation to those with whom you are acquainted. Consider inviting neighbors, friends, work associates, relatives, your dentist, service station attendant, hairdresser, store clerk, and other general acquaintances.

This may involve a personal visit, a telephone call, or a handwritten or engraved invitation. More impersonal methods that have been used are handbills, which are designed to advertise the types of groups available and invite the public to call in or attend a one-evening organizational meeting. Others have placed signs, similar in size to a For Sale sign, in their front yard advertising the meeting.

I have found that a relaxed, nonthreatening approach is the best. Say something like this: "Sue, I am having a small group meeting in my home on Tuesday evenings, and I want to invite you to come try it out. There are several of us studying together the life of Jesus in the Gospels.

We are looking for things to help us in dealing with everyday issues of life. I would like you to be a part of the group. Come this Tuesday night, and if you think it's for you, I'd like you to keep coming. If it doesn't meet your need for now, that's OK too. What do you think?"

Every small group needs to have evangelism as its emphasis; otherwise it can become a clique or closed society, and visitors will be viewed as intruders. Here are several ways to begin new groups:

1. Empty-chair principle. Each group should have an empty chair in its circle at each meeting. The chair should be filled at the next meeting as group members invite others to attend. Your group should pray each week for God to lead someone to the next meeting. As the group grows by this process it will eventually multiply and divide to form a new group.

2. Sometimes existing group members, or others who desire to belong to a study group, cannot attend the existing group because of scheduling or location conflicts. This means it's time to form a new group.

3. Invite individuals from church interest lists, newly baptized members, visitors to church, former members, friends, work associates, and others that come to mind.

4. Conduct a revival or evangelistic reaping meetings, and invite those attending to form small group Bible studies.

5. Whenever you have one person who desires to study the Bible, form a small group and invite others. Remember, two people can begin a small group! Being small is not a reason not to begin. The Holy Spirit and personal invitations will cause your group to grow.

The First Night

As a leader, you will probably feel some tension on your first night. This is normal, but remember that you are a child of God. He has asked you to speak for Him. Those whom God calls He also empowers. When you are empowered, God will melt away the tension and replace it with relaxation and words from Him. As a public speaker for the past 25 years, I can attest to God's victories in ministry. Two promises that I have found helpful are:

"Do not be anxious about anything, but in everything, by prayer and petition, with thanksgiving, present your requests to God. And the peace of God, which transcends all understanding, will guard your hearts and your minds in Christ Jesus" (Phil. 4:6, 7, NIV).

"For God has not given us a spirit of fear, but of power and of love and of a sound mind" (2 Tim. 1:7, NKJV).

On the first night, have your assistant leader and host (if you have one) meet early with you. Once the room is prepared and the details are in order, have a season of prayer together. The basic preparation would include:

- Turning on the outside house lights if it is dark outside.
- Arranging extra chairs in a circle.
- Having extra Bibles on hand.
- Having plenty of Bible study guides and extra pencils.

It is key to make everyone feel relaxed when you begin your small group meeting. I like to say something like this:

"I'm really glad to see each of you here tonight. As you know, this is a Christian small group, and we meet together for friendship, fun, and learning how the Bible can help us in our everyday lives.

"I want each of you to feel relaxed and not be on edge. Just be yourselves. You are not going to be asked to do or say anything you don't want to do. Some of us have never studied the Bible before, and that is OK. We all have to begin sometime. If you need help finding a chapter and verse in the Bible, I will help you. Someone had to help me when I first began. We will pray in the group, but I will pray and later on if some of you want to pray that is OK too. When it comes to reading, if you like reading out loud you can. If you don't like to read, that is fine—some of us do and others don't. In other words, we are all different, and we want to respect the privacy and differences of each other. How does that sound?

"Let's begin by getting acquainted with one another. I will see how good I am at remembering everyone's name. Sitting beside me is Sue Matthews. Sue is my neighbor down the street, and we have been friends for a couple years. This is Bob Case. Bob and I roomed together in college. This is Tom Ish. I met Tom last week at the grocery store, and we started talking. I invited him to stop by tonight. This is Doris Thurman. Doris is a friend from work. OK, now that we at least have heard each other's names, let's see if you can remember them. Let's take a few minutes and see how well we do.

"Next week we will talk more about what we will do in our group, but tonight I will briefly explain what we usually do. There are three basic parts to the meeting. When we begin we have what we call a *sharing time*. During this time we talk about what has happened in our lives since we last met. We usually have a question also that helps us to get better acquainted with one another. The second thing we do is our *study time*. In our case I am suggesting we use the study guides, *Face to Face With Jesus*, along with our Bibles. There are 13 lessons, so it will take us about three months to complete the study guides. Last, we talk about our personal needs or concerns, and I will lead us in *praying* for the items. As I previously mentioned, I or Bob, my assistant, will do the praying, and if some of you want to pray you can. There is no pressure on anyone to pray. How does that sound to you? Any questions or comments?

"Let's begin our meeting together tonight so you will understand better what a meeting is like. Next week we will discuss where we meet, when we meet, how long to meet each evening, your ideas about the format, et cetera. I want all of us together to decide and agree about the details of our small group."

After this, begin the group and be ready to discuss the group covenant at the next meeting. The first few meetings, make sure the members are relaxed, and that they feel that their input is important. The key is to pray, do your best, be friendly, and keep smiling.

The Second Meeting

At the next meeting, welcome everyone back. If there are any new people, introduce them to the group. Review the same thoughts you shared at the previous meeting and then give everyone a copy of the group covenant to go through together. Some leaders like to discuss the details of the covenant without handing it out, then once it is discussed they hand it out and let the members fill it out. However, some leaders do not use a printed sheet. They simply have the discussion and agree verbally.

Especially discuss what day your group will meet; the best time for the meeting; how much time to spend on the three sections of sharing, Bible study, and prayer; and whether preparation is expected outside of the group. Agree to call if you cannot attend the group meeting; discuss inviting new people and the goal of multiplying the group; also have the members write down the name and phone numbers of the leader, assistant leader, and host.

Because some may not be acquainted with the Bible, explain some of the basics. Don't ask if anyone needs an introduction; just assume someone does. Show the book list in the front of the Bible, including the page numbers to locate each book. Explain about the Old and New Testaments. Demonstrate how to locate a book, chapter, and verse.

After a few meetings, when the group members are fairly relaxed with one another, the group leader needs to introduce the concept of conversational prayer. Remember that public prayer makes many people nervous. They are afraid of sounding foolish, of not knowing what to say, or of being judged by others. Fear of praying will disappear as a group learns the basics of praying together. Tell your group members that no one will be pressured to pray. If they want to pray, they can at their discretion. The key is to speak to God with openness of heart.

There are several guidelines to follow to teach your group to pray together.

1. As a leader, model how to pray by praying first. After the leader prays, others will continue. Remember you might need to explain what prayer is to someone. Recently I was visiting with a woman who began sharing with me some of the problems in her life. The opportunity was there for me to pray with her. I asked if it would be OK if I prayed. She responded affirmatively. I bowed my head and began to pray. After I had said several words she interrupted me. I opened my eyes, and she was looking at me with a quizzical look on her face. She said, "Kurt, what are we supposed to do when we pray? I have never prayed before." I explained to her how to pray, and we began again. When I finished she said, "That is the most beautiful thing anyone has ever done for me." Don't take it for granted that everyone knows how to pray!

2. Don't spend too much time sharing prayer requests. Pray for the needs of the group. If another group member wishes to pray for the same item or need, he/she may, or simply say "Amen" as the individual concludes their prayer.

3. Select one topic at a time as your group is learning to pray together. Some groups have a three-pronged prayer. First the members begin by praising and thanking God in prayer. Second, the members pray about needs outside the group (friends, events, situations, etc.). Third, the group prays for needs within the group (family, self, fellow group members, the group, etc.).

4. The group should next pray for the "empty chair" to be filled by a new group member.

5. The group can conclude by saying the Lord's Prayer together. Saying the prayer together gives every group member an opportunity to pray. Many members will not know the Lord's Prayer. Copies should be made available for each member.

Review the section on prayer in groups in a later chapter for further assistance and ideas.

Problems in Groups

The telephone rang. It was my pastor friend Dave. Dave told me that some of the group leaders in his church wanted some assistance in dealing with conflicts between group members and how to keep the group on track. He had shared some ideas, but it was decided that a leader's meeting on the topic would be helpful. A few weeks later we met and had an excellent discussion together. Here are some of the ideas and concepts we discussed that night.

Wouldn't it be nice if life were trouble-free! Our small groups are like our families. In the group, members share about themselves—how they are feeling, the issues of life that are causing both positive and negative experiences, and their need for caring, understanding, and support. When you bring varied personalities together on a regular basis, there is bound to be some conflict.

Almost every problem in a group arises from six areas of group life. These areas are expectations of group members; participation of members in group life; the content of the meeting; the group leader's leadership skills; following the details of the group covenant; and the interaction of the members together.

1. *Expectations.* Every member of a group brings expectations in their minds of what the group should be like. Those expectations are reflected in what they perceive to be the purpose of the group; the benefits they should receive personally; what they as an individual have to offer the other group members; and how the leader should conduct the group. If these issues are not discussed in the first few weeks of group life, the group is setting itself up for conflict. A group covenant will help to solve this issue.

2. *Participation.* Because every person is in a different stage of growth all through life, and because issues of daily life cause a positive and negative effect upon those various stages, group members may be a support or a challenge to the leader. Most groups will have some individuals who are challenges. A normal group may include those who are quiet, highly verbal, aggressive, or academic; it may include a jokester, a doubting Thomas, a counselor, a counselee, and one who appears to be sleeping most of the time (you could probably add to this list). Every one of these individuals can frustrate the group and its leader now and then. A person who has something to say on every topic will probably be analyzed by the counselor and cause most to wish they wouldn't talk so much. The group leader should point out that the group members will be different from one another and they need to be respectful and accepting of one another.

3. *Content*. Sociologists tell us that there are four basic learning style audiences. There are those who believe that the core of the group should be fellowship; others will believe that studying should be the focus; another will want the group leader to function almost as a teacher by depending upon the leader for the success of the group; and action-oriented people will be frustrated by sitting in a circle and talking. Because expectations differ, the group should discuss these four areas and agree upon what is an acceptable balance in the group meeting. It is the leader's responsibility to remind the group to assist him/her in keeping on track.

4. *Leadership*. Dependence upon the Holy Spirit is the number one prerequisite of a group leader. However, not understanding group dynamics or being unaware of or ignoring issues that are causing conflict can hamper the effectiveness of the Spirit. It should be a priority of every group leader to read a few books on groups or attend a training seminar. In addition, being an assistant leader or participating as a group member before becoming a group leader will go a long way toward making life easier for the leader.

It is essential for the group leader to deal with obvious conflict in the group. The sooner conflict is dealt with, the healthier the group will be. The leader needs to talk to individuals outside of the group if necessary and let the group discuss the issues. Group members need to be able to say "I am sorry," and they need to be able to say and live the statement "You are forgiven." Conflict in a group has to be dealt with sooner or later. It will eventually destroy a group, and then the members have to deal with the pieces—so why not deal with conflict as soon as it arises.

All groups go through growth stages, similar to a child growing up or a new Christian growing in their spiritual life. These stages are birth (infant), child (toddler), youth (learning life), and adult (mature, understanding, and accepting). If the leader and members understand these stages of growth and bonding, it assists them in understanding one another. For example, one member may still be in the child stage, while another is in the adult stage of Christian growth, and the way they relate to the group will reflect their growth stage.

5. *Covenant*. If a group does not have a covenant, or if the covenant is not followed by the group, then there is sure to be trouble. For example, suppose someone is a sporadic attendee and the group never knows if they are coming. If the members have agreed to call the leader if they are to be absent, then the leader can gently remind the offender. If a group has a tendency to spend more time on the sharing segment of group life

than agreed upon, then the leader has leverage to keep them on time; otherwise the group needs to change their agreement.

The covenant gives authority and permission for the leader to lead the group. Without it there is not group ownership of the details of group life, and the leader and members may become frustrated.

6. *Group Interaction*. The group leader will not be able to control the way the members think or act toward one another. Individuals with chronic problems or those who dominate the group negatively may "put a wet blanket" over the positive interaction of the group. The leader needs to be aware of the way the members relate to each other and if necessary deal with the negative. Always have the group pray for one another and for their group relationships during every prayer time.

Problem Solving

Neal McBride suggests a four-step strategy in dealing with problems that I have found helpful.* It is not profound, but it works!

1. *Recognition* of the problem by the group. For example the leader or a member can say "I sense you are upset" or "We need to deal with this difference of opinion." Let the person or persons talk about it. The group members need to make sure that the final solution is a win/win one whenever possible. The members must learn to disagree and still love and respect one another.

2. *Personalization* of the problem. Let the group understand that difficulties are normal and it is the group's issue too, because the group is family. The leader should put everyone at ease and assist the group in solving the problem together as a unit without blaming anyone in particular whenever possible.

3. *Clarification*. The problem needs to be discussed and the issue clarified. Sometimes the problem is camouflaged by actions or reactions that are simply smoke screens.

4. *Resolution*. Select the best alternatives and put them into action.

Here are some typical problems and some suggested solutions to them.

The Chronic Problem Person. There are some individuals that have problems that they cannot seem to overcome, and their continual raising of the issue disrupts the group process. The solution is to assist the individual in receiving professional assistance or placing them in a group that deals with the issues they are struggling with.

A New Person Joins the Group. A new person who has not journeyed with the group can feel as though they don't belong. In addition, the other members may not share as openly as they did previously. The solution is to take time in the first two meetings and allow everyone to tell "their story" so that everyone is better acquainted. If the new person never seems to fit, the group leader should talk to them, and say "I sense you are not comfortable in the group" or "Are you comfortable in the group?" Allow the person to express themselves. It may be necessary to assist them in joining another group.

A Member Verbally Attacks Another's Comments. The leader should interrupt tactfully and affirm the right to disagree, but remind everyone to be kind and respectful of one another. Talk about it with a smile upon your face.

A Group Member Is Constantly Negative. The leader or other members can talk to the person about it outside of the group.

Side Discussions. If two individuals are always making comments to one another that no one else can hear, the leader should talk with them outside of the group, or redirect them to the group.

The Quiet Participant Versus the Talkative One. The group must always respect the personalities of the members, but the group also needs to be reminded from time to time that there should be opportunity for everyone to talk. Looking at a quiet person can sometimes encourage them to talk. I have discovered that the best solution for the talkative person is for the leader to take them aside and tell them that both you and they enjoy talking, and that you want them to assist you in getting others involved. Discuss possible approaches and enlist their assistance.

There are many other issues that may come up from time to time, but the areas covered should assist the group in being able to handle most problems. The regularly scheduled leader's meeting is a time when the group leaders and pastor can discuss in depth these issues and support one another.

Dave and Sally have been small group leaders in their church for almost six years. The group was originally started following a Revelation Seminar in their church in Washington State. There were some members of the church who had a vision that a small group would be perfect for nurturing the newly baptized members and to continue studying with those who had not yet made decisions. Dave agreed to be the leader, and the rest is history. Two individuals were baptized as a result of their first year of meeting. The group continues to meet with the goal in mind of reaching the unchurched.

Dave says that, with a busy schedule, it is easy to become simply nurture-centered and to neglect to keep on inviting those who are not church members. However, once the members of a group assist someone in accepting Jesus and being baptized, they want the experience to continue! If Dave's group can make it with busy lifestyles, then you and I can do the same.

---

* Neal McBride, *How to Lead Small Groups,* p. 104.

Chapter Twelve

Decisions for Christ in Small Groups

"Kurt, I need some help. Can you tell me how to obtain decisions for Jesus and baptism in a small group? I have several people in my group who have grown in their relationship with Jesus, and I think they are ready to accept Him as Saviour, but how do I approach them? Do I hand out decision cards as is done in an evangelistic reaping meeting? That seems awkward to me. Do you have any suggestions?" Sharon's question to me at the training seminar I was conducting in Portland, Oregon, is an often-asked question and an extremely important one!

One must always remember that it is the Holy Spirit who brings conviction and prepares someone for making a decision. Men and women using methods are simply tools or avenues through whom the Holy Spirit chooses to work. It is part of God's plan to use you and me in partnership with Him in what Ellen White calls the "science of soul winning." Our goal is to be aware of the Spirit's working in someone's life and be available to assist them in the decision they are making.

According to what we have learned in previous chapters, every small group should be involved in outreach, either directly by inviting non-Christians to the group; through outreach projects outside of the group; or through the activity of the task groups (Martha groups) we read about. Because every group will be involved in the lives of non-Christian people, it is imperative that the Christians in the group be aware of the basic issues in assisting someone in responding to the work of the Holy Spirit in their lives.

Studying the life of Jesus and learning how He interacted with people is our first step to follow. Philip Samaan has an excellent book on this topic entitled *Christ's Way of Reaching People*. Also, Ellen White's statement in *The Ministry of Healing* is a classic on this point: "Christ's method alone will give true success in reaching the people. The Saviour mingled with men as one who desired their good. He showed His sympathy for them, ministered to their needs, and won their confidence. Then He bade them, 'Follow Me.' "*

As one can see, establishing relationships—understanding the needs of people, getting acquainted with them as individuals—was the first step of Jesus. This is the natural setting of the small group dynamic. That is why the first priority of the leaders and Christian group members should be developing relationships and winning the confidence of others in the group. This is done more effectively if the members of the group do activities together with other members outside of the group. I have helped members rototill their gardens and gone to ball games with them.

The leader also needs to be aware of the personal needs of the members. Many times personal problems or concerns are a priority over biblical material and what one has learned. Sarah, a member of one of my groups, was convicted that she should worship on the Sabbath, but her first concern was not how she understood what the Bible said, but which denomination had the best children's program. Once the needs of her children were met, Sarah was willing to think about other issues.

Also, not everyone in your group will grow spiritually at the same speed. It is necessary to be aware of signs regarding where your members are spiritually so they can receive the necessary care and attention. This requires listening to comments and watching body language. For example, if someone says, "I can see how Jesus could make a difference in my life," that member is expressing a positive affirmation for Christianity. If they have never accepted Jesus into their life, then they should be visited outside of the group and given an opportunity to accept Jesus.

I believe the best way to establish a small group ministry in a local church is to put in place an evangelism process that involves small groups, reaping crusades, seminars, pathway events, et cetera. I suggest that the church establish a small group ministry and visitation plan to establish individual Bible studies or to place interests in small groups. Eventually a reaping crusade can be conducted. The newly baptized and the nonbaptized interests can be placed in small groups. These groups meet weekly, and are ideal for establishing new members and for a continual follow-up to reap those not yet baptized. In addition, groups for developing friendships and used as pathway groups or stepping-stones to Bible study groups or church attendance can be a key part of the strategy.

In addition, these new members have a network of friends and relatives that they can invite to the small groups. Through the groups and reaping crusades the cycle continues. Those who have addictions and other special personal needs can be placed in support groups and given the extra care needed. I believe this type of evangelism cycle assists in "closing the back door of the church" to the loss of new members.

Several years ago I taught a Revelation Seminar. At the end of the seminar we placed the interests in a small group that met in a home under my leadership. We studied the major doctrines of the Adventist Church. The group included Fred, my assistant leader; Tom and his wife, Sarah, who belonged to another Protestant denomination; Joe, a Catholic; Bill, who belonged to an interdenominational church; another Seventh-day Adventist, Jeanne; and me. (The names have been changed, but all other details are accurate.)

Our group chose to study the major doctrinal teachings of Scripture. Each evening the group members would take the study guide home and review it for the next group meeting. The night we were studying the Sabbath, Joe came to the group meeting all excited. He told the group, "I can't believe it! I have been worshiping on the wrong day for more than 60 years!" He looked at Bill and said, "Isn't it amazing, Bill? We have been going to church on the wrong day!" Bill looked at Joe and said, "I haven't been going on the wrong day! I disagree with you." Thus followed an interesting discussion for the evening that I began by reminding the group that we must disagree in love and respect of one another and their views.

How did I respond as a group leader to this situation?

1. I visited Joe outside the group and affirmed his decision about the Sabbath. I gave him literature to read and invited him to church the next Sabbath. He came and eventually was baptized.

2. I also visited Bill outside the group. I wanted to make sure that the differences of opinion hadn't dampened his spirits or hurt his feelings. We discussed his feelings and prayed together. He kept coming and told me he knew that the group members cared about him.

3. During one group meeting Tom said that he believed Saturday was the Sabbath. Sarah, his wife, didn't say much, but I could tell that she was not in agreement and was troubled. I visited them outside the group meeting and discussed their feelings. They began attending church on both

Saturday and Sunday. Tom wanted to be baptized as an Adventist, but Sarah didn't want to. We continued to work with them.

When group members accept Jesus, make significant spiritual growth steps, and have major victories in their lives, the group needs to affirm their decisions and victories. As you can see, sensitivity, awareness, and visitation outside of the group is necessary in order to assist the members in their lives.

Four Levels of Decision

I have also found it helpful to have the group leaders and assistants understand the levels of decision that individuals think through in their minds. When these are understood, the leader can be aware of where the member is in the decision-making process. The levels are as follows:

Level One: *Information Level*. It is on this level that the person gathers information and data. They accumulate facts about Jesus or a particular teaching of Scripture. If the individual does not have all the information they need to answer the questions about a particular subject, then they will not be ready to make a decision on that topic.

Level Two: *Conviction Level*. Once the individual believes they have enough information on a given subject and that all their questions have been satisfactorily answered, they are in a position to begin thinking about the implications of what they have learned. The Holy Spirit begins moving upon their mind and life. The person begins to wrestle with what they should do with the new information and experience.

Level Three: *Desire Level*. Once the individual begins to think about the benefits of a potential decision, they will consider doing something with the facts they have learned. If I ask a person privately if they can see any benefits in accepting Jesus or a doctrine in their life, and they tell me no, sometimes a personal testimony will get them thinking about the benefits.

Level Four: *Action Level*. Once a person has progressed through the first three levels, they are ready to make a decision. I ask them, "Is there any reason you can think of that you couldn't accept Jesus today?" If they give me a reason and they still see the benefits of a positive decision I usually say, "If we clear up this issue of [whatever their objection is], will you then be ready to make a decision?" This helps to prevent their putting their decision off until a later time.

Group members need to understand these levels, because it assists in determining where a person is in making a decision by simply listening to their comments during the group meeting. For example, in the story about Joe and Bill, Joe progressed quickly through each step and was ready to act, but Bill was still wrestling with the first level. It is usually best to discuss decision-making privately with group members as they develop spiritually at their own pace. However, always be ready to affirm any member who makes a public decision during the group time. In addition, if someone makes a decision, ask them to share it during the next group meeting so the entire group can rejoice and thank God together.

The key is to listen, observe, affirm, visit, and ask questions one-on-one for the most positive results.

The Hispanic church in Gladstone, Oregon, has made small groups a key strategy. The members are spread out over a wide distance. This makes it difficult for the members to come together for a long reaping series several nights a week. Currently, small groups in several locations are studying doctrinal material. Decisions are made in the groups. In addition, every few months a weekend reaping rally calling for decisions is conducted by the pastor. These rallies are followed by a short series of reaping meetings at other times during the year. Currently 18 individuals have been baptized through this strategy.

---

* Ellen G. White, *The Ministry of Healing* (Mountain View, Calif.: Pacific Press Pub. Assn., 1905), p. 143.

Chapter Thirteen

I'm a Group Leader —Now What?

I was told recently that we need to have a "little extra fat on our bones" to make the best small group leaders. I discovered that the word FAT was an acronym for F = faithful to God; A = available to meet the needs of the group members; T = teachable and willing to learn. I really like that definition!

Expanding upon the above acronym, the following qualifications are helpful in group leaders.*

An Understanding and Commitment to Spiritual Principles. First Timothy 3:6 and 5:22 state that church leaders should not be novices in the Christian life. Spiritual leaders must first understand Scripture and be experienced themselves.

A Growing Relationship With Jesus. If a leader is to model spiritual growth and encourage others, it must first be a reality in their own life. A developing Christlike character must be evident. Several times New Testament Epistles encourage God's children to "grow in the grace and knowledge of our Lord and Savior Jesus Christ" (2 Peter 3:18, NKJV).

A Commitment to Care for People. The leader is dedicated to reaching out to the members of the group and demonstrating loving concern for their personal sorrows, joys, and needs. In addition, it is essential that the leader be an encourager to assist the members in their personal growth and development.

A Passion for Winning Lost People to Jesus. The number one reason for the existence of the church is to connect people with Jesus. A leader must have this burning desire.

A Student of the Bible. The group leader needs to enjoy studying and learning about the Scriptures on a daily basis. A leader cannot facilitate a scriptural study if they do not study themselves.

A Teachable Person. A leader may not know very much about leading a group at first, but if they are humble and willing to learn, they have the necessary ingredients for success.

A Desire to Serve Others. Jesus said that true leadership is putting the needs of others first. The leader also models what they are teaching by being a living example—an authentic Christian.

Time Commitment. It takes time to be a group leader. The leader must be willing to spend one night a week in a group meeting; attend a regularly scheduled leaders' meeting; prepare for the weekly meeting; and make sure the members' needs are being met. Of course, there is the assistant leader and in many cases other Christian group members to assist in meeting the needs of the group members outside the group time.

There are other characteristics of a group leader, but these are basic. One must keep in mind that none of us meet all of these characteristics as perfectly as we would like, but Jesus has promised us strength and the power of the Holy Spirit.

Motives for Leadership

As one reflects on the characteristics for leadership in a small group, the bottom line is motive. Correct motives that allow the leader to serve positively are the following:

- A desire to uplift and glorify God.
- A desire to please God in using the spiritual gifts given to you.
- A desire to do something positive for God's church.
- A desire to share with others the fact that Christianity can meet one's personal needs.
- A desire to connect lost people with Jesus Christ.

Incorrect motives can lead to the demise of a group and in some cases destroy the spirituality of the members. Motives that destroy group life are:

- A desire to fulfill an emotional need, such as acceptance, approval, etc.
- A desire for power or authority over others.
- A desire to fulfill a personal imbalance of approval and admiration (a "look at me" complex).
- A desire and need to be always in the center of whatever is happening.

The bottom line is that the leader should desire to assist the group in reaching its goals and fulfilling its purpose for existence. If the leader's reasons for participating are incorrect, they should not serve in this capacity.

Functions of a Leader

As the leader serves the group members there are several functions that are basic to positive leadership: a. A successful group leader seeks to develop personal relationships with each member of the group. This goes beyond knowing their first name and a casual "Hi, how are you?" It involves spending quality time with them and attempting to understand their unique contribution to the group. b. A successful group leader is sensitive to the needs, feelings, and personalities of the members, and affirms their individuality. c. A successful group leader continually models love, trust, and acceptance as normal behavior for Christians. d. A successful group leader will truly be a facilitator and guide the flow of the discussion and attempt to involve all group members in a nonthreatening manner. e. A successful group leader encourages members to listen to, accept, and respect those with a view that differs from the leader or members. f. A successful group leader assists the group in accomplishing its goals and growing into a mature Christian community.

Stages or Cycles of Group Life

Small groups go through stages of development just like people. It is essential that leaders understand this process. One five-stage model uses the terminology of infancy, toddler, child, youth, and adult. Another six-step model uses the terms pre-contract stage, orientation stage, power and control stage, trust stage, change stage, and conclusion or new beginning stage. However, the terminology I prefer is:

- Exploration Stage: The members are just beginning with the group. They are asking such questions as "Do I belong?" "What is expected of me?" "What can I expect from others?"
- Transition Stage: The members are more comfortable with one another and are beginning to venture out and "test the water" to see if the group is a safe place to belong. The members begin to relax and enjoy one another.
- Action Stage: The group members are comfortable with one another. They are very open in sharing their personal opinions and have developed trust and acceptance.
- Termination/New Beginning Stage: The group is ending; dividing into two groups; or beginning a new set of study guides or estab-

lishing a new purpose for existence. The members usually feel sad that change is interrupting their established bond, but they adjust and move on to a positive new group experience.

One must remember that stages are a part of life. If a leader is aware of these stages and the emotions that the group members experience, he or she can talk to the group about it and the members will adjust more quickly.

Leadership Styles

Understanding what is expected of you as a leader is indispensable in order for you to fulfill your job description. In addition, your attitude, methods, and behavior—that is, how you operate—will also determine your ability to facilitate a group. Let's take a look at the various leadership styles and which seem to be best for small group leadership.

Traditionally there are four basic leadership styles. These are autocratic, authoritative, democratic, and laissez-faire.

An *autocratic* leader is domineering and dictatorial. They attempt to be in total control, with members as listeners and followers. The leader determines policy and wants the group to choose the leader's personal goals for themselves. They often make decisions unilaterally and disregard other viewpoints. The group members are almost puppets.

An *authoritative* leader has a definite direction in mind, but is open to the ideas of others. The leader usually has strong control, yet the members are actively involved in discussing the leader's goals and ideas. The leader is open to modification based on group input, but usually does not change his or her personal goals for the group. This type of leader uses his or her personal power to involve others.

The *democratic* leader is group-centered, and shares control with the group. The leader is assertive, yet values the abilities and opinions of others. This style of leadership creates a sense of security and belonging in the group. All policies, goals, and guidelines are a matter of group discussion, and the goal of the leader is to obtain group ownership and participation.

The *laissez-faire* leader is one who is permissive and passive. There is minimal control by the leader. The members direct the group meeting. The leader doesn't prepare, and lets things drift. The leader appears to be passive and doesn't seem to care. This style provides fragmentation and encourages indecisiveness.

Which of the traditional styles is best? I think that almost everyone would agree that each style at times has a place and usefulness, but most people prefer the democratic style. There are, however, two other styles that need to be considered: servant leadership and situational leadership.

The *servant leadership* style arises from Luke 22:24-30. The disciples of Jesus were arguing about who was the greatest. Jesus said to them, "The kings of the Gentiles exercise lordship over them, and those who exercise authority over them are called 'benefactors.' But not so among you; on the contrary, he who is greatest among you, let him be as the younger, and he who governs as he who serves" (verses 25, 26, NKJV).

Jesus also said, "If anyone desires to be first, he shall be last of all and servant of all" (Mark 9:35, NKJV). Jesus then demonstrated to the disciples what He was saying when He took the role of servant and washed their feet (John 13:5), something the disciples evidently felt was beneath their dignity. Even though Jesus, the King of the universe, had the right to demand to be waited upon, He demonstrated that a true leader is one who earns respect and loyalty by the way they treat people. Servant leaders do not demand their own way, do not try to maneuver politically to get their own way, and, most important, do not "walk over people," or stretch the truth to accomplish their own purposes. Servant leaders put the desires and needs of others first. They earn respect because of their sincerity, commitment and honesty, love and respect of others, and desire to build up others.

Jesus exemplified true servant leadership when He gave His life for His followers. This is true servant leadership! The apostle Paul, in an attempt to explain this concept of being a servant, wrote, "For though I am free from all men, I have made myself a servant to all, that I might win the more; and to the Jews I became as a Jew, that I might win Jews; to those who are under the law, as under the law, that I might win those who are under the law; to those who are without law, as without law (not being without law toward God, but under law toward Christ), that I might win those who are without law; to the weak I became as weak, that I might win the weak. I have become all things to all men, that I might by all means save some" (1 Cor. 9:19-22, NKJV).

Paul was an educated man and a strong leader, but he did not demand; he served. This does not come naturally. However, by yielding to the grace and power of Jesus Christ, we become servant leaders who reflect the style of Jesus.

Over the past several years a new concept called *situational leadership* has emerged. Situational leadership means that the style of leadership will vary depending upon the situation and circumstance. For the Christian this means that servant leadership must always be the fundamental style; but sometimes the leader is given, by permission of the followers, the right to be more directive when needed.

Here is an example of this in group life. The members of one group covenant to begin at 7:00 p.m. and end at 9:00 p.m. But they always seem to start late and go overtime. This frustrates some of the members, who give the leader permission to be autocratic with them and assist them in fulfilling their agreement. The leader keeps the group on time, but does it with a smile on their face and a kind spirit.

The choice of leadership style is key to a group that is enjoyable, as opposed to one that no one wants to belong to. In addition, a servant leadership democratic style develops new leaders. I was visiting a church and consulting with the group leaders. I was impressed with the leadership effectiveness and personality of Sally, one of the group leaders. I asked about her after the meeting and was told that she was at one time an ECR person—extra care required to be around her. Sally's attitude, insecurity, and bitterness made those around her miserable. However, the love, kindness, and acceptance of the group members and the desire of the group to serve her—to love her just as she was—was used by the Holy Spirit to make a difference in her life.

Sally's story is the result of servant leadership. Because she was served, Sally now serves. That is what ministry is all about!

---

* Neal McBride, *How to Lead Small Groups,* pp. 29-31.

Chapter Fourteen

Tips for Success in Small Groups

Last week my telephone rang, and the caller asked me a very important question: what did I consider to be the essential ingredients for a small group program to succeed? There are many things that come to mind, and I will probably leave someone's number one item off the list, but here are several to consider, not in any particular order.

1. *Establish a relaxed atmosphere*. If you want your group members to return each week, then the small group atmosphere must be relaxed. Your group should be fun. No one wants to feel stressed and out of place in a group meeting. The purpose is to make people feel needed and glad to be there; to feel as if they are at home.

Make sure your group members know it is OK to be themselves and to come as they are. Assure them that no one in the group will ever intentionally be put on the spot or asked to do something they are not comfortable in doing. The group will not go around the circle for talking, reading, or prayer. The meeting will be voluntary as members choose which parts to participate in.

2. *Establish some ground rules*. This is usually called a covenant. Within the first couple meetings, the group should agree on what day it will meet; the time to meet; the amount of time to spend on sharing, Bible study, and prayer. It should discuss the do's and don'ts. The idea is to have group ownership of the details of group life. This is essential to assist in group attendance, morale, multiplying the group, and having a basis by which to evaluate group life.

3. *Have a regular leaders' meeting*. The small group leaders,

assistant leaders, and hosts need support and continual training. Because of this a regularly scheduled leaders' meeting is essential—weekly at first, and eventually once a month.

The pastor should be present at the leaders' meeting at least once a month, even though there may be a member who is coordinating the small group program. If the pastor is not available, the lay leader should lead. This assists the leaders in realizing the importance of the group ministry. There are three agenda items for each meeting: a. Vision casting, which is done by the pastor. The leaders need to be continually reminded of the church's need and support of small groups. In addition, they need to realize how important they are to the church's vision and goal of reaching unchurched people for Jesus. b. Sharing time: the leaders need to "huddle" together and talk about their concerns, joys, heartaches, and frustrations, and pray with one another for support and encouragement. As leaders they are fighting against Satan and his attacks against those who need to make decisions for Jesus and grow in Him. It is easy to become weary in the battle on the "front lines." In addition, this is a time for the leaders to fill out written reports about group attendance and how things are going in their groups. c. Skill training is another essential part of the meeting. The leaders need to be continually growing in their abilities of ministering to those in their group. A little time at each meeting will be a tremendous assistance in this equipping ministry.

4. *Secure the commitment of the senior pastor.* It is critical that the church family and the leaders realize that small groups are a priority to the pastor. The pastor should be involved in the regular leaders' meetings, and in one of the groups. He or she should talk about groups during the worship service, and print the group leaders' names in the church bulletin or newsletter.

5. *Make small groups a priority over program.* An indicator of how important groups are to the local church will be in how it plans daily church life for the church members. A heavily packed church diet of many programs and committee meetings will keep many church members from group participation. The members have only so much time. They cannot be expected to support programs and myriads of committees, have their jobs and family responsibilities, and still be part of a small group. The local church must decide its priorities, or they will burn out everyone, and daily church life will be a burden and discouragement.

6. *Focus on outreach.* Every group must be outreach-focused, or group life will eventually stagnate, and the group will die out. Focusing

upon other people is critical to keeping the group vibrant and active. There is no greater joy than connecting unchurched people to Jesus Christ. When the group realizes their group is helping people find Jesus, the small group ministry in the local church will survive and thrive!

These are several essentials that will keep your church's endeavor to establish a small group ministry alive and growing. Let me share a story with you.

Several years ago a small outreach group in central Oregon began studying the book of Revelation. The group met for many months. Whenever they finished with one set of study guides, they would begin a new group. This went on for almost two years. I asked the group leader, Barry, what was the secret to maintaining the excitement over such an extended period of time. He beamed at me and said, "Kurt, when you see members of your group learning about Jesus, accepting Him as Lord and Saviour, and becoming baptized members of your church, it gets in your blood! There is no greater joy than growing and learning in Jesus and helping others know Him. When you see and experience this, you are impelled by the Spirit to keep sharing. You can't stop! This is what Jesus has called us to do."

Jesus has called us to connect people to Him! That is the ultimate purpose of life. When Jesus returns at His second coming He won't ask us whether we were the top shoe salesman, or owned the most buildings in town, or chose the best investments, or sat on the most church committees; He will ask us if we used our gifts, talents, and abilities in leading lost people to Him. What will your answer be?

Chapter Fifteen

Where Is It Working?

What should a small group ministry look like? Some feel that there is only one way to develop a small group ministry. Others feel that the shape of a small group ministry should depend upon the spiritual gifts, needs, and personalities of the church members, which will differ from one congregation to another. We addressed these issues to some degree in an earlier chapter, and I will let your local church decide how God is speaking to them after a time of study, prayer, and fasting. What I want to do is share with you several strategy ideas that are followed by others and then suggest a couple models for the future.

There are four basic models being followed in the Seventh-day Adventist Church, with a fifth coming on the scene. These are (1) the basic program-based church with several small group options added for those who desire to participate; (2) a program-based model of church life in which every member is encouraged to belong to a group, and every ministry is encouraged to set aside time for group life (for example, the choir, the children's division leaders, the music committee, the literature committee, et cetera, should have a time for small group interaction at least once a month); (3) a program-based church that has decided that they want to become a small-group-based church, or at least to let programs take second place to small group life; (4) a church with Sabbath school action units. In addition, there are a few churches (5) who are planning, dreaming, and even trying to start a pure cell-based church that has no programs but only small groups, along with a weekly worship service.

Let's take a look at examples of each.

Program-based Church With Small Groups as an Option

The Vancouver, Washington, church has an active church program. Church members are leading in health seminars such as cooking schools, a Vacation Bible School, spiritual gifts seminars, photography classes, and other outreach programs. The 460-member church considers small groups to be a necessary part of church life, especially for newly baptized members and for ongoing outreach. There are usually three to eight groups available in the church, including ongoing groups for Bible study and for reclaiming and obtaining decisions. Following reaping meetings, the groups are used especially for newly baptized members. In addition, fellowship groups are especially appreciated by the singles and retired members of the church. The members enjoy the groups and use them as a nonthreatening place to invite their friends.

Program-based Church Aiming at Groups for Every Member

The Kelso-Longview church in Longview, Washington, began a small group ministry in 1993. It is a church of 470 members, with approximately 300 in attendance. The church currently has 23 small groups with 210 group members. The groups are used as a nurturing and reclaiming avenue for the church family. However, the goal is to be outreach-focused, and several individuals have been baptized, along with a few nonattending members who now have returned to church. Following a series of reaping meetings the newly baptized are integrated into small groups to assist in the assimilation process into the church and in their continued spiritual growth.

A Program-based Church Becoming a Small-Group-centered Church

Klamath Falls, Oregon, is a 313-member church close to the California border. The current pastor has given strong leadership in small groups to his congregations for many years. Small groups are the center of church life, but the outreach strategy includes other options as well. Some of these are individual Bible studies and reaping meetings. As a major result of a combination of small outreach groups and a reaping crusade, 72 baptisms have occurred in the first eight months of this year. The church will end the year with approximately 18 small groups, including some studying doctrines, the Gospel of John, and Philippians.

The strategy is to nurture the new members and to encourage them to invite their friends and family members to the small groups and other church outreach programs. The goal is to make small groups the center of outreach and nurture.

Sabbath School Action Units

In the 1980s the Michigan Conference began an intensive endeavor to involve every active church member in a small group experience involving outreach through the Sabbath school class. These classes are called action units. The rationale is that these action units will fulfill Ellen White's counsel regarding the purpose of Sabbath school. Action units have been used around the world as a tool for soul winning and nurture—or as one of my friends says, to "catch and keep."

Action units are organized with 10 key elements.

1. Size: six to eight, for optimum participation.
2. Leadership: each class has an outreach leader called a care coordinator, who is an assistant to the church personal ministries leader. Assisted by a secretary, the care coordinator promotes outreach in accordance with the class plan.
3. Planning: the outreach plans of the class are developed immediately after class organization at a special planning session.
4. Time: an hour minimum is provided to the class. Twenty-five minutes is devoted to caring and outreach at the beginning of the class, followed by 35 minutes for Sabbath school lesson discussion.
5. Nurture: there is weekly caring for missing class members. Members contact those who are sick, missing, etc., during the week.
6. Sharing: each week the members share their outreach experiences and discuss plans for the coming week.
7. Study: the Sabbath school lesson is reviewed and discussed by the class members.
8. Leader development: there is a monthly leaders' meeting similar to what has been shared in preceding chapters. Once a month the class leaders meet with the personal ministries leader, Sabbath school superintendents, and pastor to discuss the coordination of the work of the classes and church.
9. Evaluation: once a month the class members meet in a member's home to evaluate and plan their continuing projects and class projects.

In some locations the action unit outreach project is weekly small groups in the homes of the members. Thus, every church member is involved in a small group experience that involves outreach.

In the Bantama district in the Africa-Indian Ocean Division, there were 1,245 baptisms in 1994; 942 were primarily from action units and 303 from public reaping crusades. There are 21 churches and companies in the district. In one church there are 90 action units.

In 1992 the church in Pendleton, Oregon, in the Upper Columbia Conference, ended the year with 92 baptisms. These were the result of individual Bible studies, home small groups, and evangelistic reaping meetings, along with Sabbath school action units being a vital part of the outreach structure. The caring outreach of the members made the difference. The pastor provided the vision, training, modeling, and encouragement; and the Holy Spirit blessed their efforts!

Cell Church

The cell church model is working in non-Adventist churches in many countries around the world. However, Adventists in North America have struggled with this model. Our church roots grow out of a program-based model, and few have challenged this traditional paradigm successfully.

A few Adventist churches are working on this model. For example, a pure cell-based church is being formed in Michigan and Texas, with plans for others in California, Oregon, and Washington. It will take a few years for these churches to produce fruit.

Models for the Twenty-first Century

I believe we will see radically new paradigms of church life in the next century. Who says, for example, that in order to be a church there must be a building? I believe that we need to plant churches without buildings. If we are serious about winning our communities for Jesus, we won't be able to afford to build enough buildings to house everyone. Why not have hundreds or even thousands of small groups, and rent an auditorium or stadium for church services? Think about the many ways we could spend the millions of dollars we invest in buildings if we rented facilities for worship and used the leftover funds for outreach! We must target specific areas of a city, do demographic studies and door-to-door surveys, provide neighborhood Bible reading programs and other programs to meet the needs of the community, establish personal relationships, begin small groups, and eventually turn homes into house churches. This will take hard work and innovation, but how else will the world be given an opportunity to know Jesus?

Another strategy is to plant targeted churches. Even in areas where an Adventist church already exists there are unchurched people or unreached cultural groups, such as particular ethnic groups, or a generation with a different subculture. Why not discover what is culturally relevant to that particular segment of the population, establish small groups among them to develop relationships, meet needs, and introduce the people to Jesus? The next step would be to develop church services and meetings that speak their cultural language. The idea that we don't need to start another church until the existing church has no empty seats ignores the fact that it might take different methods to reach different people.

I like the sound of what is being called the 20/20 plus class for Sabbath school. Every member belongs to a small group during the week (either a task group or home group), and meets together on Sabbath morning for Sabbath school. The meeting is divided into five parts: a group building exercise in the beginning; group worship, which includes singing and prayer; Bible study, which is inductive with life application; equipping or skill-building exercises to assist in equipping the members for ministry; and ministry action plans, developed for group members to use in sharing the gospel with their friends and neighbors.

My Personal Vision

To be faithful to Scripture and Ellen White, small groups cannot remain an optional part of church life. Small groups must become part of the major focus around which the other events of the church revolve. The small group evangelizes, nurtures, and supports the members in their ministry. One advantage of this paradigm is that a pastor would be able to oversee multiple churches more easily, because the church members are ministering to the group members.

I believe there is more than one way to organize a church that is centered on small groups. *One* way is to take an existing program-based church and streamline the activities of the church to accommodate a small-group-based ministry. It may be that everyone has a 20/20 plus Sabbath school class or an action unit to which they belong. There would be home-based small groups during the week in addition to ministry or task groups that meet. There are some people—"Marthas"—who prefer to be active and do ministry rather than sit in a circle and study during the week. Such a "Martha" group can still sit together on Sabbath mornings for Sabbath school and meet periodically for ministry planning, prayer, and Bible study.

A *second* paradigm would be to divide up the agenda of the small group. The prayer, fellowship, and Bible study occur at various times during the week. The small group Sabbath school class could be where the Bible study occurs. There could be a fellowship or social meeting after the church service, or sometimes during the service, in which the members sit in a circle and share their personal experiences and what they have gained in Bible study, and pray together. During the week they would be involved in outreach of many types in using their spiritual gifts. Those with similar outreach functions, which include home small groups, would meet as a group for planning, prayer, support, and doing ministry.

A *third* paradigm is one that includes everyone in a home-based small group. The church has no programs except for an occasional training weekend, ministry rally, youth rally, etc. Every person in the church belongs to a small group that meets during the week. All ministry functions of nurture, support, caring for the discouraged and sick, outreach to seekers, etc., occurs during the week in the groups. The groups come together on Sabbath morning for worship and Sabbath school.

A *fourth* small group model that intrigues me is the one in which there is no church building. Personal door-to-door visitation, needs-based events (parenting seminars, health seminars, etc.), are done in the neighborhoods in a community to begin small groups. These groups become house churches that meet on a weekly basis. Several home groups may form one house church. These house churches would then periodically all get together in a rented facility for worship services, ministry rallies, etc. This could happen once a month. Sometimes the youth from several of the house churches may get together for special events. I have a vision of entire communities having house churches every few blooks. If we truly reach the world in latter rain proportions with the outpouring of the Holy Spirit we must think beyond what exists. *We must have churches without walls in our communities.*

A *fifth* model is an existing program-based church that decides to plant a new cell-based church. Through a door-to-door visitation program, mailings, community events, personal need seminars, reaping crusades, etc., Bible studies are started in the community. The newly baptized members and others who are studying are organized into small groups. The city is divided into regions. Each region has a leader. The regional leader oversees up to 10 groups. Once the number of groups in a region rises above 10, a second leader is added to the region.

The church members from the original church become the group leaders in their neighborhoods in their region. As the groups grow with new members, new leaders are trained within the group. Eventually the number increases, and a new small group or cell-based church is begun.

The possibilities are exciting! However, a note of caution is needed. It is necessary to dream and plan, but it could be detrimental to attempt radical paradigm shifts within existing program-based churches. In fact, Jesus cautioned against putting new wine into old wineskins. My counsel is to move existing churches slowly into a small group program. For the radical changes, start new churches where small groups are normative. Well-intentioned leaders sometimes become martyrs for a good cause by choosing the wrong battle. God does not want church fights over structure and methods; He wants ministry to be accomplished. Can changes be made? Yes, but in wisdom, prayer, and unity of the local church body.

Dan had a vision that God wanted him to start a small group in his home that targeted members in their early to late twenties. These were members who never came to Sabbath school, arrived at church late, and many times never bothered to attend at all. His study group dealt with issues that spoke to their needs such as how to be a Christian in the workplace, or how parents can impart spiritual principles to their children. The young adults loved it! Eventually some of them invited their friends and the group grew. Eventually Dan asked permission to teach a Sabbath school class. Permission was granted, and he invited his small group to attend his class. Today 12 to 20 young adults who were staying home many Sabbath mornings are now coming to Sabbath school and church on a regular basis and inviting others!

Chapter Sixteen

The Bones Will Stop Rattling

When I was a boy some of the most exciting words to me were "Let's go camping!" I loved to camp. I lived in the desert and I loved the mountains—the smell of the pine and fir trees; the sound of the creek splashing over the rocks; the crackle of a fire as it licks the dry wood and sparks shoot heavenward; the chipmunks and squirrels—and don't forget the fishing.

I was born with a fishing pole in my hand. I would get up at any time in the morning or drop anything, including my baseball glove, when the word "fishing" came up.

I was 10 years old and in my glory—we were camping in the mountains—and the fishing was supposed to be terrific. We got up at sunrise and began the mile and a half hike—mostly uphill—to what was touted to be the hottest fishing hole on the mountain. I was excited! Pine and fir trees, darting chipmunks, the sun beginning to peek over the hill—this was life at its best! I determined that I was going to live here permanently when I grew up. I followed my dad, fishing pole in hand. Those first few hundred feet, my dad kept telling me to slow down, for in my excitement I would stab him in the back with my fishing pole. As the distance increased, I began to slow down. My dad would look over his shoulder and shout words of encouragement to me, such as "Hurry up, Kurt—what's taking you so long? I thought you wanted to go fishing!" Finally with perspiration streaking down my face, my muscles aching and feeling like jelly, I called ahead and said, "Dad, can't we rest? I'm tired." He looked at me with a smile on his face and said, "Kurt, I thought you liked the mountains." I replied, "I do, Dad, but not this kind of mountain!"

Four men snake their way up the side of another mountain. The trip has been long. The hour is late. A level place on the hillside is reached, and they sit down. They are tired. Their muscles ache. Perspiration is streaming down their faces. They look over at Jesus as if to say, "Lord, we like mountains, but not this kind of mountain."

Twilight is settling over them—they long to rest and to sleep, and three of them do, but the fourth sits, thinking and praying. Jesus brought Peter, James, and John with Him to pray, as He did again later in the Garden of Gethsemane. But instead of praying, they sleep. Jesus, however, is wide awake. He takes off His sandals and rubs the sore spots on His feet. He looks over at His sleeping followers. They don't seem to understand. He speaks of suffering, they think of conquering. He speaks of sacrifice, they think of celebration. They think they see—think they hear—but they don't.

Jesus has given His best, but sometimes His followers don't seem to understand His passion. He is on earth to connect the lost to His Father. He wants to make His disciples fishers of men and women, not fishers of fish! As Jesus considers the road ahead of Him—the Garden of Gethsemane, the abuse of the crowd, His death on the cross—He begins to pray. As He prays, the Father hears and answers. We read about it in Luke 9:28-36:

"Now it came to pass, about eight days after these sayings, that He took Peter, John, and James and went up on the mountain to pray. As He prayed, the appearance of His face was altered, and His robe became white and glistening. And behold, two men talked with Him, who were Moses and Elijah, who appeared in glory and spoke of His decease which He was about to accomplish at Jerusalem. But Peter and those with him were heavy with sleep; and when they were fully awake, they saw His glory and the two men who stood with Him. And it happened, as they were parting from Him, that Peter said to Jesus, 'Master, it is good for us to be here; and let us make three tabernacles: one for You, one for Moses, and one for Elijah'—not knowing what he said. While he was saying this, a cloud came and overshadowed them; and they were fearful as they entered the cloud. Then a voice came out of the cloud, saying, 'This is My beloved Son. Hear Him!' When the voice had ceased, Jesus was found alone. But they kept quiet, and told no one in those days any of the things they had seen" (NKJV).

Verse 28 says that Jesus took Peter, James, and John up on the mountain to pray. In order to be prepared for ministry, and the temptations and tragedies of everyday life, one must pray! Peace, power, and wisdom come only by prayer.

Verse 29 states that as Jesus prayed His face was altered. He is connected with the Father. The circumstances of His life did not change; Jesus still had the cross, the Garden of Gethsemane, and the abuse of the crowd to face. His prayer did not change the situation; it prepared Him to face it. His face is changed not because He is free of the difficulties, but because through prayer He has received strength and power to triumph over trials. Prayer prepares you and me for ministry!

Verse 32 says that Peter, James, and John slept heavily. They are "down for the count," as we say—they are snoring. But as they sleep, the glory of God lights up the hillside like daylight! They are startled awake, and see Jesus transfigured, and His face glowing, because He is connected to the Father in prayer and He reflects His divine glory! The Bible states that the disciples saw the glory of God. God took them up on the mountain to experience His glory, but instead they only saw it.

Although the experience was no doubt life-changing for the disciples, can you imagine what it would have been like for them if they had been awake and praying with Jesus? The question for you and me today is Are we a recipient of God's power, or only a spectator? Are we asleep on the sidetracks of life when we should be praying? God wants your life and mine to be Spirit-filled.

When they came down off the mountain, the disciples were unable to cast a demon out of a possessed child. Jesus told them their lack of power was caused by a lack of faith, and that this kind of faith comes only through prayer and fasting.

Jesus is very clear. An empowered church is a church full of power-filled lives, and power-filled lives come only when we are a people of prayer!

Come back to the valley with me—Ezekiel's valley. God told Ezekiel to say to the dry bones of the church—you and me—"Hear the word of the Lord!" "I will cause breath to enter into you, and you shall live. I will put sinews on you and bring flesh upon you, cover you with skin and put breath in you; and you shall live. Then you shall know that I am the Lord." " 'I will put My Spirit in you, and you shall live, and I will place you in your own land. Then you shall know that I, the Lord, have spoken it and performed it,' says the Lord" (Ezekiel 37:4, 5, 6, 14, NKJV).

Just as Jesus was changed by the Spirit of God on the mountain, so we will be changed and altered to reflect God's image when through prayer we are connected to Him. Satan does not want God's church to stand upon its feet as an empowered army to win the world to Jesus Christ. Satan does not want God to fill you or me with His Spirit. But God will do so, when we humbly and sincerely give our entire being to Him. When we fully and completely belong to Jesus; when we do and go where He wants us to go; when lost people mean more to us than our businesses, our houses, our possessions—then we will enter the kingdom of heaven. *When this occurs the bones will stop rattling. It will be impossible for them to rattle. They will be connected—connected through the Spirit.*

Prayer and fishing for souls—we need to become truly committed to these two activities. God has given us the commission and the steps to empowerment. Will we listen? I believe we are listening! I have faith in our God, and I have faith in you, and in what God will do in you and in me. The Bible says that He who began a good work in you will finish it! This is not maybe or perhaps. It is a sure thing!

Yes, when you and I enter the land that Ezekiel talked about—God's land for you and me: heaven—the bones will no longer rattle. Not because God's Spirit is no longer present, but because, as He says, I "have spoken it and performed it" (verse 14, NKJV), I have fully and completely filled you with My Spirit.

The bones have stopped rattling—I can't hear them. Instead I hear angel voices, I hear trumpets, I hear the voice of Jesus! "Even so, come, Lord Jesus!"

Small Group Weekly Report

Group____________________ Area __________ Meeting date__________

Leader ____________________ Assistant leader ____________________

Host ____________________ Location ____________________

Names of those in attendance

1. __________	11. __________
2. __________	12. __________
3. __________	13. __________
4. __________	14. __________
5. __________	15. __________
6. __________	16. __________
7. __________	17. __________
8. __________	18. __________
9. __________	19. __________
10. __________	20. __________

Please mark each name with a code: L = leader; AL = assistant leader; H = host; V = visitor; RV = Return Visitor; R = regular attender; M = local member; N = nonlocal member; NS = non-SDA.

Starting time for your group meeting _______ Stopping time __________

Did you use: praise songs? _______ Conversational prayer? __________

Empty chair? ____________________

Rate the quality of your group experience this week (1-10). __________

If less than 5, why? ____________________

Do you need to talk with the pastor? ____________________

Please use the back of this sheet for: (1) praise reports; (2) problem areas; (3) information pastor needs to know about yourself and people you are working with; (4) answered prayers.

BIBLIOGRAPHY

Anderson, Leith. *A Church for the Twenty-First Century*. Minneapolis: Bethany House Publishers, 1992.

Arnold, Jeffrey. *The Big Book on Small Groups*. Downers Grove, Ill.: InterVarsity Press, 1992.

Barker, Steve, et al. *Good Things Come in Small Groups*. Downers Grove, Ill.: Intervarsity Press, 1985.

———, et al. *Small Group Leader's Handbook*. Downers Grove, Ill.: InterVarsity Press, 1982.

Barna, George. *Evangelism That Works*. Ventura, Calif.: Regal Books, 1995.

———. *The Power of Vision*. Ventura, Calif.: Regal Books, 1992.

Beckham, Bill. *The Two-winged Church Will Fly*. Houston: Touch Outreach Ministries, 1994.

———. *The Second Reformation*. Houston: Touch Publications, Inc., 1995.

Burrill, Russell. *A Biblical and Adventist Historical Study of Small Groups as a Biblical Mission*. Berrien Springs, Mich.: Andrews University, 1996.

———. *Revolution in the Church*. Fallbrook, Calif.: Hart Research Center, 1993.

Cerna, Miguel Angel. *The Power of Small Groups in the Church*. Newbury Park, Calif.: El Camino Publishing, 1991.

Davis, Deena. *Discipleship Journal's 101 Best Small Group Ideas*. Colorado Springs, Colo.: NavPress, 1982.

Finnell, David. *Life in His Body.* Houston: Touch Publications, Inc., 1995.

Galloway, Dale, and Kathi Mills. *The Small Group Book.* Grand Rapids: Fleming H. Revell, 1995.

George, Carl F. *Prepare Your Church for the Future.* Tarrytown, N.Y.: Fleming H. Revell, 1991.

——— and Warren Bird. *The Coming Church Revolution.* Grand Rapids, Mich.: Fleming H. Revell, 1994.

Green, Michael. *Evangelism in the Early Church.* Grand Rapids, Mich.: William B. Eerdmans Pub. Co., 1970.

———. *Evangelism Then and Now.* Downers Grove, Ill.: InterVarsity Press, 1979.

Hamlin, Judy. *The Small Group Leaders Training Course, Participant's Manual.* Colorado Springs, Colo.: NavPress, 1990.

———. *The Small Group Leaders Training Course, Trainer's Manual.* Colorado Springs, Col.: NavPress, 1990.

Hestenes, Roberta. *Using the Bible in Groups.* Philadelphia: Westminster Press, 1983.

Hipp, Jeanne. *How to Start and Grow Small Groups in Your Church.* Monrovia, Calif.: Church Growth, Inc., 1989.

Hunter, George G. III. *How to Reach Secular People.* Nashville: Abdingdon Press, 1992.

Icenogle, Gareth Weldon. *Biblical Foundations for Small Group Ministry.* Downers Grove, Ill.: InterVarsity Press, 1994.

Jacks, Bob, and Betty Jacks. *Your Home a Lighthouse.* Colorado Springs, Colo.: NavPress, 1986.

Johnson, Kurt. *Small Group Outreach.* Hagerstown, Md.: Review and Herald Publ. Assn. 1991. Kreider, Larry. *House to House.* Houston: Touch Publications, Inc. 1995.

McBride, Neal F. *How to Build a Small Group Ministry.* Colorado Springs, Colorado: NavPress, 1995.

———. *How to Lead Small Groups.* Colorado Springs, Colo.: NavPress, 1990.

Navigators. *How to Lead Small Group Bible Studies.* Colorado Springs, Colo.: NavPress, 1982.

Neighbour, Ralph W., Jr. *Where Do We Go From Here?* Houston: Touch Publications, Inc., 1990.

Peace, Richard. *Small Group Evangelism.* Downers Grove, Ill.: InterVarsity Press, 1995.

Samaan, Philip G. *Christ's Way of Reaching People.* Hagerstown, Md.:

Review and Herald Pub. Assn., 1990.

Schilt, W. Clarence. *Dynamic Small Groups.* Hagerstown, Md.: Review and Herald Pub. Assn., 1992.

Williams, Dan. *Seven Myths About Small Groups.* Downers Grove, Ill.: InterVarsity Press, 1991.

Williams, Garrie F. *Ministerial Continuing Education.* Silver Spring, Md.: General Conference Ministerial Association, 1991.

Wollen, Albert J. *Miracles Happen in Groups Bible Study.* Glendale, Calif.: G/L Regal Books, 1976.